First World War
and Army of Occupation
War Diary
France, Belgium and Germany

48 DIVISION
Divisional Troops
48 Sanitary Section
1 June 1915 - 31 March 1917

WO95/2753/1

The Naval & Military Press Ltd
www.nmarchive.com
Published in association with The National Archives

Published by

The Naval & Military Press Ltd

Unit 10 Ridgewood Industrial Park,

Uckfield, East Sussex,

TN22 5QE England

Tel: +44 (0) 1825 749494

www.naval-military-press.com

www.nmarchive.com

This diary has been reprinted in facsimile from the original. Any imperfections are inevitably reproduced and the quality may fall short of modern type and cartographic standards.

© **Crown Copyright**
Images reproduced by permission of The National Archives, London, England, 2015.

Contents

Document type	Place/Title	Date From	Date To
Heading	48th Division BEF 48th Mobile Vety Section Mar 1915-Oct 1917 To Italy		
War Diary	Nieppe	01/06/1915	26/06/1915
War Diary	Busnes	27/06/1915	30/06/1915
Heading	48th Division 121/6439. Summarised but not copied 121/6439 48th Divl. Sanitary Section Vol IV From 1st To 31st July 1915		
Heading	War Diary O.C. Sanitary Section, 48th (S.M.) Division from 1st July 1915 To 31st July 1915 (Volume 4)		
War Diary	Busnes	01/07/1915	01/07/1915
War Diary	Lillers	02/07/1915	19/07/1915
War Diary	Terramesnil	20/07/1915	20/07/1915
War Diary	Authie	21/07/1915	31/07/1915
Heading	48th Division Summarised but not copied 121/6754 48th Sanitary Section Vol V August 1.15		
Heading	War Diary of O.C. Sanitary Section, 48th (S.M.) Division. from 1st August 1915 to 31st August 1915 (Volume 5)		
War Diary	Authie	01/08/1915	10/08/1915
War Diary	Bus Les Artois	11/08/1915	31/08/1915
Miscellaneous	48th Division. Enteric Group.		
Miscellaneous	48th Division Infantry Section.		
Heading	48th Division Summarised but not copied 121/7183 48th (S.M.) Sanitary Section Vol VI Sept 15		
Heading	War Diary of O.C. Sanitary Section. 48th (S.M.) Division from 1st September 1915 To 30th September 1915 (Volume 6)		
War Diary	Bus	01/09/1915	30/09/1915
Heading	48th Division Summarised but not copied 121/7449 48th Div. Sanitary Sect. Oct. 15 Vol VII		
Heading	War Diary O.C. Sanitary Section, 48th (S.M.) Division 1st October 1915 to 31st October 1915 (Volume 7)		
War Diary	Bus.	01/10/1915	31/10/1915
Heading	War Diary. of O.C. Sanitary Section, 48th (S.M.) Division. from 1st November 1915 To 30th November 1915 (Volume 8)		
War Diary	Bus.	01/11/1915	30/11/1915
Heading	War Diary of O.C. Sanitary Section 48th (S.M.) Division, from 1st December 1915 to 31st December 1915 (Volume 9)		
War Diary	Bus	01/12/1915	31/12/1915
Heading	War Diary of O.C. Sanitary Section. 48th (S.M.) Division from 1st February 1916 To 29th February 1916 (Volume XI)		
War Diary	Bus.	01/02/1916	29/02/1916
Heading	War Diary of O.C. Sanitary Section 48th (S.M.) Division. from 1st March 1916 To 31st March 1916 (Volume 12)		
War Diary	Bus	01/03/1916	26/03/1916
War Diary	Couin	27/03/1916	31/03/1916

War Diary	Bus	31/03/1916	31/03/1916
Heading	War Diary of O.C. Sanitary Section 48th (S.M.) Division. from 1st April 1916 to 30th April 1916 (Volume 13)		
War Diary	Couin	01/04/1916	30/04/1916
Miscellaneous	A.D.M.S. 48th Divn.	11/04/1916	11/04/1916
Miscellaneous	Prefecture de la Somme.		
Heading	War Diary of Sanitary Section 48th (S.M.) Division From 1st May 1916 to 31st May 1916 (Volume 14)		
War Diary	Couin	01/05/1916	31/05/1916
Heading	War Diary of O.C. Sanitary Section 48th (S.M.) Division. from 1st June 1916 to 30th June 1916 Volume 15		
War Diary	Couin	01/06/1916	30/06/1916
Diagram etc	A. Fly-Proof Latrine for deep trench 3/4 Front view.		
Heading	War Diary of O.C. Sanitary Section 48th (S.M.) Division. from 1st July 1916 to 31st July 1916 (Volume 16)		
War Diary	Couin	01/07/1916	16/07/1916
War Diary	Bouzincourt	17/07/1916	28/07/1916
War Diary	Le Plouy	29/03/1916	31/03/1916
Heading	War Diary of O.C. Sanitary Section 48th (S.M.) Divn from 1st August 1916 to 31st August 1916 (Volume 17)		
War Diary	Le Plouy	01/08/1916	09/08/1916
War Diary	Beauval	10/08/1916	13/08/1916
War Diary	Bouzincourt	14/08/1916	28/08/1916
War Diary	Bus	29/08/1916	31/08/1916
Heading	War Diary of O.C. Sanitary Section 48th (S.M.) Divn from 1st September 1916 to 30th September 1916 (Volume 18)		
War Diary	Bus	01/09/1916	10/09/1916
War Diary	Beauval	11/08/1916	17/09/1916
War Diary	Bernaville	18/09/1916	30/09/1916
Heading	160/1788 48th Divl Sanitary Section. Oct 1916		
Heading	War Diary of O.C. Sanitary Section 48th (S.M.) Division. from 1st October 1916 to 31st October 1916 (Volume 19)		
War Diary	Henu	01/10/1916	21/10/1916
War Diary	Doullens	22/10/1916	23/10/1916
War Diary	Baisieux	24/10/1916	31/10/1916
Heading	War Diary of O.C. Sanitary Section 48th (S.M.) Divn from 1st November 1916 to 30th November 1916 (Volume 20)		
War Diary	Baizieux	01/11/1916	30/11/1916
Heading	War Diary of O.C. Sanitary Section 48th S.M. Division from 1st Dec. 1916 to 31st Dec 1916 (Volume 21)		
War Diary	Warloy	01/12/1916	31/12/1916
Heading	140/1947 48th Divl. Sanitary Section. Jan 1917		
War Diary	War Diary of Sanitary Section 48th Division from 1-1-17 to 31-1-17. Vol 22		
War Diary	Warloy	01/01/1917	09/01/1917
War Diary	Hallencourt	10/01/1917	31/01/1917
Heading	War Diary of O/C Sanitary Section 48th (S.M.) Divn. from 1st Feb to 28th Feb. 1917 (Volume 23)		
War Diary	Mericourt	01/02/1917	03/02/1917
War Diary	Cappy	04/02/1917	28/02/1917

Heading	War Diary. of O.C. Sanitary Section-48th (S.M) Division. from March 1/1917 to March 31/17. (Volume 24)		
War Diary	Cappy	01/03/1917	25/03/1917
War Diary	Peronne	26/03/1917	31/03/1917

48TH DIVISION

BEF

48TH MOBILE VETY SECTION

MAR ~~APR~~ 1915 - ~~MAR 1919~~ Oct 1917

to ITALY

Army Form C. 2118.

WAR DIARY
or
INTELLIGENCE SUMMARY.
(Erase heading not required.)

Instructions regarding War Diaries and Intelligence Summaries are contained in F.S. Regs., Part II. and the Staff Manual respectively. Title pages will be prepared in manuscript.

Place	Date	Hour	Summary of Events and Information	Remarks and references to Appendices
NIEPPE	1/6/15		Section inspecting & assisting knels. 1 case German Measles. Arranged with mayor of NIEPPE for more frequent street cleaning and refuse removal – Badly needed. Military authorities to contribute 20 francs per week. — Obtained O.C.'s sanction for same.	
"	2/6/15		Interviewed S.S.O. re supply of disinfectants of which there is shortage. Section as above. Baths at PONT NIEPPE cleaned & whitewashed by section. Visited refuse tip at ARMENTIERES with O.C. San. Sect. 9th DW = Regim'l office. 2 cases German Measles. Meeting of M.O.s at A.D.M.S. office	
"	3/6/15		Section as above.	
"	4/6/15		" " Filthy ditch – main sewer of NIEPPE – at S.W. corner of Place de l'Eglise causing great nuisance.	
"	5/6/15		" " Inspected billets at PONT NIEPPE vacated by 9th DW = v. Bad.	
"	6/6/15		" " Will discuss. inspecting 1/4 RS R.G.A. Lectured write duty men of cyclists. Billet of 9th DW = Signal Section – filthy.	
"	7/6/15		" " Arranged with D.C.I 2nd S'n F.A.M.B. to dispose of house refuse collected at PONT NIEPPE by covering with earth. Arranged cleaning of food ditch in NIEPPE. Took N.C.B. to see refuse tip at ARMENTIERES.	
"	8/6/15		" " To ARMENTIERES re refuse tip. Arranged with O.C. Sanitary Section 2nd DW. to report to higher authority on gravity & urgency of the matter. Inspected entire trenches with S.M.R.G.M.G. 1st No 33rd PG Bde N.R. 1/8 R. War. Reg. ? ENTERIC. Meeting of M.O.'s at A.R.M.S. office. Interviewed O.C. San. Section 12th DW. 2 cases German Measles.	
"	9/6/15			
"	10/6/15		" " Testing water will Horrocks apparatus borrowed from 12th DW = San. Section. Took O.C. to ARMENTIERES to meet D.C. San dec. 27th DW = to aforementioned refuse tip. Changed pools in PLOEGSTEERT Wood with Paraffin.	
"	11/6/15		" " Will A.D.M.S. to visit A.D.M.S. 27th DW. more water testing.	
"	12/6/15		" "	
"	13/6/15		" " ? ENTERIC – 914 J after W.H. King 1st F Coy, S.M. R.E. – investigated.	
"	14/6/15		" " Arranged with mayor to restrain inhabitants from throwing house refuse into street. Confirmed arrangement with him to notify earlier infectious disease.	

1577 Wt. W10791/1773 500,000 1/15 D.D. & L. A.D.S.S./Forms/C. 2118. 9 elsewhere.

WAR DIARY
or
INTELLIGENCE SUMMARY.
(Erase heading not required.)

Army Form C. 2118.

Place	Date	Hour	Summary of Events and Information	Remarks and references to Appendices
NIEPPE	15/6/15		Section inspected & assembled. Inspected several detained premises & found very bad conditions, refuse, flies, improper urinals arranged & visits to have visited all latrines in area.	
"	16/6/15		Section as above. With D.A.D.M.S. to farms just behind left trenches — made recommendations & elaborates.	
"	17/6/15		Section as above. Arranged to train Green School G.O.C.'s billet & Not mess. Visited farms with interpreter re clearing manure from yards — generally practicable — a great improvement. Cesspit, tank & pump cart to 13th & 15th Divs: STEENWERK	
"	18/6/15		Section as above. Consultation with O.C. San: Sec: 13th Divs: re D.W. in the area.	
"	19/6/15		" " " But will D.A.D.M.S. POPERING:	
"	20/6/15		" " "	
"	21/6/15		" " Visited Mobile Hygiene Lab.	
"	22/6/15		" " With regards to civilian cesspits, many of which were found to be swarming with flies — the mayor will have them treated with chloride of lime & we will supply it. He will cause manure to be removed from farms & billets in NIEPPE. Water samples. N.O. + meeting at A.D.M.S office. D.W. preparing to move.	
"	23/6/15		" " Handed over cesspit cart & pump to San: Sec: 12th Div.	
"	24/6/15		" "	
"	25/6/15		Preparing to move. Section hauling mill walk with manure evening — greatly hampered by onset of wet weather.	
"	26/6/15		Handing over to San: Sec. 12th + Canadian Div. Case ? Dip:[?]theria.	
BUSNES	27/6/15		Moved to BUSNES. Château & grounds in filthy condition left by 9th D.W. Hundreds of uncovered cesspits among its crowded Reported.	
"	28/6/15		Working at château.	
"	29/6/15		Cleaning château. PATHOMELBY BILLETS. Left over night.	
"	30/6/15		Preparing to move. Visited Red Cr number of men detached to Btns with A.D.M.S.	

General sanitation of D.W.'s had become quite good prior to move from NIEPPE. Chief remaining dangers were of civilian making. Flies not very numerous yet — hope fly safers will be erected in sufficit — it would be a good investment. Water carts difficult to work — Horrocks listing apparatus been suffit [?] urgently needed. No serious infectious diseases [?]

S

July/15

48th Division

121/6429.

Summarised but not copied 121/6439

48th Div'l: War Diary Lectr

Vol IV

From 1st to 31st July 1915.

Confidential.

War Diary

O.C. Sanitary Section, 48th (S.M.) Division.

from 1st July 1915 to 31st July 1915.

(Volume 4)

WAR DIARY or INTELLIGENCE SUMMARY

Army Form C. 2118.

(Erase heading not required.)

Place	Date	Hour	Summary of Events and Information	Remarks and references to Appendices
BUSNES	1/1/15		Moved from BUSNES to LILLERS – Measles reported at HURIONVILLE – billet of 4th & 6th Bn Gloster Regt – visited same – also Town Major of LILLERS. Detached 2 men with Thresh disinfectors to 1st Rest Station for Lice-Scabies work.	
LILLERS	2/2/15		Section working at H.Q. & inspecting units. – Visited D.C. No 6 Mobile Lab. (Hygiene) re local waters. Visited men detached at Bde H.Q.	
"	3/2/15		Section as above. Visited O.C. Mobile Lab – Hygiene & Bacteriological.	
"	4/2/15		? Diphtheria at HURIONVILLE – investigated. Visited 6th Warwicks at AUCHEL & arranged pail latrine system – no more general available.	
"	5/2/15	"	Arranged for exam. of water at H.Qrs ? testing of chlorination result in H.Q. water cart. Visited all detached men. Inspected Mobile Vet. Section.	
"	6/2/15	"	Arranged for exam. of water at AUCHEL & testing of 6th Warwick Cart. Lecture to section. Inspected Gloster Div. Cav. Well M.D.	
"	7/2/15	"	"	
"	8/2/15	"	To HURIONVILLE & LILLERS. Arranged for earlier exam at BURBURE also water cart 6th Worcester.	
"	9/2/15	"	Cerebro-Spinal Meningitis Fever (1 case) & one German measles (? S.F.) in 8th Worcesters at BURBURE. Arranged for exam. of Wales at LOZINGHEM also water in cart of 7th Warwicks.	
"	10/2/15	"	Arranged for exam. of water at Examinal BEQUET–LILLERS – No 3 tree.	
"	11/2/15	"	To LAPUGNOY – billets of 4th R. Berks – case of ? Enteric Typhoid, arranged for exam. of blood & water. To AUCHEL to arrange disinfection of Army platoon of 6th Warwicks.	
"	12/2/15	"	Disinfected verminous platoon at AUCHEL – visited Examinal there to enquire about ? infection or plate for A.P.M. To NOEUX-ex MINES will DADMS to see O.C. San. Sec. 47 Div. which we are to relieve.	F. Dale Croft DADMS

WAR DIARY
or
INTELLIGENCE SUMMARY.
(Erase heading not required.)

Army Form C. 2118.

Places	Date	Hour	Summary of Events and Information	Remarks and references to Appendices
LILLERS	13	7/15	Section on duty. Lecture & section	
"	14	7/15	" Visited Bde. H.Qs at NOEUX-LES-MINES, HOUCHAIN & LES BREBIS with C.S.O.2	
"	15	7/15	" Disinfecting machine & the 2 men returned from Div¹ Rest Station - closed	
"	16	7/15	" Lecture to section. Experiment with manure incinerator at H.Qs	
"	17	7/15	" " " "	
"	18	7/15	" Clearing up at LILLERS preparatory to move.	
"	19	7/15	" Marched to BERGUETTE - entrained for DOULLENS - marched to TERRAMESNIL	
TERRAMESNIL	20	7/15	Terrible state & plague of flies - place recently vacated by French Troops - marched to AUTHIE.	Sanitation of area has been
AUTHIE	21	7/15	Section on duty - inspecting and supervising. Detached 1Cpl & 2 men to Corps HQ at MARIEUX - inspected same with C in C commandant. Inspected River AUTHIE with R.P.M. with view to river conservancy.	over from French. Very good incinerators in villages and bullet-left
"	22	7/15	Section as above. Visited trenches at HEBUTERNE - arranged to continue French system of Refuse removal & incineration & refuse from village & adjacent trenches,	and bullet-left, generally very
"	23	7/15	" Disinfecting machine to Div¹ Rest Station at SARTON. Inspected 2nd Fd Co Lean inside R.E. & 5th Warwicks at COURCELLES - Detached 6Cpl + 2 men to BUS-EN-ARTOIS. but L cops of Detached 1 Cpl & 2 men to HEBUTERNE - & 1 man to SAILLY-AU-BOIS - all to supervise stone manure sanitation.	letters everywhere outside their dwellings latrine
"	24	7/15	" Visited trenches along whole front of Div¹ - visited 143rd & 145th Bdes.	arrangements
"	25	7/15	" Visited Bde HQs with SRQMG arranged to continue the French system of deep midden latrine with close fitting wooden covers in trenches - Bdes to issue orders authorising fatigue parties for same or R.E. to deeply covers.	flies, latrine offices, latrine arrangements a very bad, except in parts of trenches

F. Dale Capt
R.A.M.C.

Army Form C. 2118.

WAR DIARY
or
INTELLIGENCE SUMMARY.
(Erase heading not required.)

Instructions regarding War Diaries and Intelligence Summaries are contained in F. S. Regs., Part II. and the Staff Manual respectively. Title pages will be prepared in manuscript.

Hour, Date, Place		Summary of Events and Information	Remarks and references to Appendices
AUTHIE	26/7/15	Section inspecting & supervising. — Inspected farm at ST. LEGER with C.R.E. — silt for proposed div. baths — inspected artillery bivouacs along river Authie. Sent through A.D.M.S. instructions to M.O.s re construction of midden latrine & trenches.	
"	27/7/15	Section as above. Visited Corps A.G.S. Threshed disinfector for low rest station to Bath at AILLY. Obtained textile supply of disinfectants owing to bad state of area generally	Sanitation of area very unsatisfactory as yet — enormous accumulations of manure everywhere. Consequent fly plague. Slow progress being made in cleaning up villages where units are billeted. But earlier labours difficult yet & burning of manure discouraged by G.O.C.
"	28/7/15	Visited COIGNEUX re 2 cases "Typhoid" removed 10 days ago. Meeting at A.D.M.S. office at M.O. of 144th Fd. Bde about going into trenches. To BUS re P.S.F. — false alarm. To HERUTERNE re water	
"	29/7/15	With A.D.M.S. to SAILLY, COIGNEUX & ST. LEGER. Visited 48th Div. Amm. Park at VAL-DE-MAISON – obtained empty cord. drums for trenches. To Corps HQ at MARIEUX. Section also collecting tins of all kinds for latrine purposes in the trenches	Trench sanitation very difficult in the low-lying section owing recent very wet weather especially as there is great shortage of latrine vessels – but the latrine accessories of the Div. is generally fairly good.
"	30/7/15		
"	31/7/15	Inspected Supply Col. at AUTHIEULE.	Practically no infectious this month. T.R.

F. Bale Capt R.A.M.C.
O.C. San. Sec. 48th Div.

48th Division
Summarised but not copied 131/6754

S

48th Sanitary Section
Vol V
August 15.

Aug 15

Confidential

War Diary

of

O.C. Sanitary Section, 48th (S.M.) Division.

from 1st August 1915 to 31st August 1915.

(Volume 5)

Army Form C. 2118.

WAR DIARY
or
INTELLIGENCE SUMMARY.
(Erase heading not required.)

Instructions regarding War Diaries and Intelligence Summaries are contained in F.S. Regs., Part II. and the Staff Manual respectively. Title pages will be prepared in manuscript.

Hour, Date, Place	Summary of Events and Information	Remarks and references to Appendices
Aug 7/15 AUTHIE.	Section inspecting, disinfecting and removing cleaning and disinfection of dirty billets, including removal of vermimous straw, manure etc.	
Aug 8/15 "	14 men of section are detached, with Corps HQr, Bde HQr and advanced Br. Hd Qr of F Amb. O.C. on leave.	
Aug 9/15 "	Section as above. Horrocks walker + staff officer arrived for tour – very welcome.	
Aug 10 "	Section " Visited COURCELLES, COLINCAMPS, HEBUTERNE & trenches of 5th Bn Glos. R.	
Aug 11 BUS LES ARTOIS	Section as above – moved from AUTHIE to BUS. TO SAILLY consulted M.O. ye adv Bde 143 State 3rd S.M.F.A re sanitation of village.	
12/15 "	Section as above. Inspected billets in BUS. Visited COURCELLES (2nd F. Coy RE) COLINCAMPS (143 Inf Bde.) COURCELLES (5th War R 4) Reinforcement No 527 Pte Smith W.D. 1/5 R. Fus. Regt arrived.	
13/15 "	Section as above. To COIGNEUX re cleaning of billets occupied up till now by French, & testing of water at spring. SAILLY. BAYENCOURT- 8th Bn Worcester sanitary man out digging with fatigue parties – OC promised not to offend again. This Bn free from lice whereas others now heavily infected – presume this is due to regular use of flowers of sulphur and paraffin – spread mixture.	2nd Lt Lewes & Morris reported for duty/Lt taken ill 10/6 respect 15/15 St Stockdale 1/3 War from Base I Robb Capt Rham &t

Forms/C. 2118/10

WAR DIARY
or
INTELLIGENCE SUMMARY.
(Erase heading not required.)

Army Form C. 2118.

Hour, Date, Place	Summary of Events and Information	Remarks and references to Appendices
14/8/15 BUS-LES-ARTOIS	Lecture re before Two men detailed to supervise cleaning of latrines.	
15/8/15 "	Lecture of COIGNEUX — detached here. To SAILLY as above. Arranged for R.W. Amm. Col. to lend staff nurses for manœuvre shifting.	
16/8/15 "	To SAILLY-AU-BOIS TERNE re prevalence of diarrhoea among troops — mostly transient — few needing evacuation with T. to food — much attributed to green apples wine & local tinned stuff? — rather worse out of trenches than in. Interviewed M.O. 1/4 S.M. 76 Warwicks re trench latrines. 1985 Pte Palmer 1/4 Oxf & Bucks L.I. ? Enteric.	
17/8/15 "	To BEAUVAL — interviewed Col. Beard RAMC, O.C. No. 8 Mobile Lab. re diarrhoea — arranged for exam. of fæces samples. To VILLERS BOCAGE — arranged for O.C. ? infect. Dis Hosp to send particulars of 48th Div. Enteric Group cases on Form attached — Appendix A. Form filled in by M.O. i/c unit. Appendix B.	
18/8/15 "	Reinforcements 214 Pte Harrington W. 1/1 Bn Lan Coy arrived & 5 Pte Porter F.C. 1/4 Bn Glouc R.	
19/8/15 "	2 Cases Measles (German) 1/1/4 Bn Glouc R. Testing well water in BUS. — to BAYENCOURT. ST. LEGER — y. ta Warwick. 2875 Pte RYDER T.F. 1/6 Bn Glouc Regt ? ENTERIC. Visited D.W. Rest Stn 2nd S.M. F.Amb re exam = of diarrhœa cases. To COLINCAMPS — 144 hf 18fdr & 1st S.M. R.F.A. Bde.	
20/8/15 "	To BAYENCOURT — M.D. 1/5 Warwicks. To MARIEUX — 7 Corps — VAUCHELLES 3rd S.M. F.Amb. 1326 Cpl Roberts 3rd S.M. R.F.A.O.C. ? Enteric.	

V. Ball Col. RAMC

WAR DIARY
or
INTELLIGENCE SUMMARY.
(Erase heading not required.)

Army Form C. 2118.

Hour, Date, Place	Summary of Events and Information	Remarks and references to Appendices
21/8/15 BUS-LES-ARTOIS	Lecture as before. To DOULLENS re hiring of Ecup't. Ferm. - Maire could only give address of AMIENS firm.	
22/8/15 "	To LOUVENCOURT. Iv'd S.H. Ft. Amb. 2156 L/c W. Vowles 1/4 Bn Glouc. R. – ? Enteric. Lecture as before. With Fly Commissn'r ADKS. to SAILLY, CORCELLES, HEBUTERNE, BAYENCOURT, COIGNEUX.	
23/8/15 "	" LOUVENCOURT, ARQUÈVES, VAUCHELLES. " No 1.8 & 9 mobile ab BEAUVAL re water and sterilizing. To trenches 4th Berks & Worcesters in good	
24/8/15 "	" AUTHIE. To Marieux – Insp'd 7th Corps HQrs well. Interviewed S.S.O. re sanit'n of coln.	
25/8/15 "	" Insp'd Div'l HQrs & 6th Gloster's, COIGNEUX village. To DOULLENS to see Rouldcomnd'g RTO re drawing enf'g'd drums & cart from Railhead. Reinforcement 790 Pte V.O.C. Fleet Plumber Bay arrived.	
26/5/15 "	Lecture as above. Insp'd Supply Col'n. To Coigneux re Latrines of French Territorials.	
27/8/15 "	" With ADMS. to 6th Glosters 4th Glosters & Coigneux. To SAILLY re inspection of wells, BOUIN – French Baths and Scabies Hospital.	
28/8/15 "	With Lt Fullon RAMC. O/C Mob Lab. Hygiene to Sample water lost at sufflier at HEBUTERNE & COIGNEUX. Insp'd 4th Worcesters. To SAILLY continuing insp'n of wells.	
	759 Pte Prenter W. 1/4 Bn Glouc. R. ? Enteric 2690 " Annial F.V. 1/5 R. War R. ? Enteric	T. Dale Capt RAMC.T.

Forms/C. 2118/10

WAR DIARY
or
INTELLIGENCE SUMMARY.
(Erase heading not required.)

Army Form C. 2118.

Hour, Date, Place	Summary of Events and Information	Remarks and references to Appendices
29/8/15 BUS-LES-ARTOIS	Section as before. To SAILLY - completing sinking & disinfⁿ of wells. Off^r & section visiting detached men, Inspecting wells.	Sanitation of area generally slowly improved.
30/8/15 " "	To HERUTERNE visiting detached men. Inspecting wells & disinf^g. 1 case German measles in 9 Sth Bn. 1457 Spr T.L. Bridgewater 1st S.M. F^d Coy R.E. ? ENTERIC. Lt Lloyd R.E. Sick leave.	Flies became less constantly being moved and human nature much less than human nature. Fly nuisance much less.
31/8/15 " "	" " Mairie of BUS re wells. C.R.E. re well protection. THIÈVRES re civilian typhoid - obtained particulars of 14 cases during last year reported.	marked largely owing to weather and cold weather experienced during month. French sanitation generally good but very difficult in low lying sectors on right owing to wet. These sectors now handed over to 48th Div? Danger to be met in the liability to pollution of the deep wells on which all villages depend for bulk of water. These all require protection but C.R.E. services get unobtainable during month - must press it. These reported. 10 Cases? Enteric reported during month but only and defn^{ly} diagnosed (typhoid) entire ford to set up fresh ... during coming autumn. N.B.

Kale Captⁿ R A m C
O.C. San.Sec. 48th Div

am trying to resist all calls cut

48th Division.

ENTERIC GROUP.

Disease.   Date of Notification.

No.   Name.   Unit.

Age.

Date of Reporting Sick.

State of health immediately prior to reporting sick – with date

Similar illness among friends or associates, or at same billets,
concurrently or previously.

Any diarrhoea, if so how long?

Is illness attributed to any particular cause?

Any untreated water taken for drinking or tooth-cleaning?

Any meals or refreshment taken not with unit – e.g. milk
at farms, beer at estaminets.

Remarks

Please forward to Sanitary Officer.
                    48th Division.

To O.C, - 48th Division Sanitary Section.

Disease.

No.   Name   Rank   Unit.

Age.   Date of Notification.
          Date of reporting sick.

* State of health just before reporting sick, with dates.
* Similar illness among his friends or associates, or at same billets, concurrently or previously. Any diarrhoea, if so how long.
* Is illness attributable to any particular cause. Exact location if possible, of billets for 14 days previous to onset.
* Any untreated water taken for drinking or tooth cleaning.
* Meals or refreshment taken not with units. e.g. milk at farms, beer at estaminets.

Have Company Cooks.-
    (1) been inoculated
    (2) had typhoid fever.

Remarks.

    * Please obtain these particulars from patients pals or associates.

48th Division

summarised but not copied 12/7/83

48th (S.M.) Sanitary Section

Sep 15

Ans

Sep 1/15

Confidential

War Diary

of

O.C. Sanitary Section, 48th (S.M.) Division

from

1st September 1915 to 30th September 1915.

(Volume 6)

Army Form C. 2118.

WAR DIARY
or
INTELLIGENCE SUMMARY.
(Erase heading not required.)

Instructions regarding War Diaries and Intelligence Summaries are contained in F. S. Regs., Part II. and the Staff Manual respectively. Title pages will be prepared in manuscript.

Hour, Date, Place	Summary of Events and Information	Remarks and references to Appendices
1 9/15 BOS.	Section doing routine work – 14 men detached as before. To DOULLENS arranging with Sub-prefect of department for removal of civilian typhoid case from THIEVRES. One case measles in 1/4 Bn Gloster Regt.	
2 9/15 "	Routine. Sanitation of No 3 Labour Bn recently attached to Div? discovered very elementary.	
3 9/15 "	Routine. Inspection of Trenches – left sector – with G.S.O.2 & C.R.E. – very satisfactory. Am getting empty oil, cresol drums & having them made into washing bowls, Mot. Amb. Workshop	
4 9/15 "	Routine. One case ? Enteric in 1/8 Bn Worcester Regt.	
5 9/15 "	Routine. Visited No 18 & 79 Mot. Lab. 6 ? One case Paratyphoid B. up in Bucks Bn Oxf. Steam disinfector arrived – 2 large chambers mounted on Foden Lorry allotted to the Div ? 3 days a week – useful. But only a slight mitigation of the lice nuisance. The cages of the chambers have no trays. These are being made by the Mot. Amb. workshop also a working platform to be attached to the side of the lorry.	Bucks L.I. This is the third case of Paratyphoid recently reported from base. All these cases left the Div? in June, one will be eczema, another will an injured ankle!
6 9/15 "	Routine. Disinfector with 2nd F? Ambulance – very satisfactory. 2 ? Typhoids at AILLY exam? by Bacteriologist. Spring at THIEVRES well exam? by O/c No ? Mot. Lab.	J. Dale Capt Rannel.

Army Form C. 2118.

WAR DIARY
or
INTELLIGENCE SUMMARY.
(Erase heading not required.)

Instructions regarding War Diaries and Intelligence Summaries are contained in F.S. Regs., Part II. and the Staff Manual respectively. Title pages will be prepared in manuscript.

Hour, Date, Place	Summary of Events and Information	Remarks and references to Appendices
7/9/15 BUS.	Routine. To Sully re civilian ? Typhoid already returned to one case typhoid reported - interpreter not long in train	
8/9/15 "	Routine. With A.D.M.S. SUZEGER. Disinfector doing 5th Warwick	
9/9/15 "	To DOULLENS arranging beds for the 2 civilian from SAILLY diagnosed Typhoid. To HEBUTERNE where M.O. Y/c Bn. in billets reports 14 cases ? Typhoid. Not very suspicious but cases removed to F.A. for observation and precautions taken.	
10/9/15 "	Wells at COURCELLES & SAILLY sampled with L.O. Y/c 9 Mob. Lab. - HEBUTERNE re ? Typhoid. Inspected Centre Trenches & sale factory. To FONQUEVILLERS re same above	
11/9/15 "	To 143 Inf Bde to arrange collection of refuse from left trenches and from FONQUEVILLERS and incineration. Furnaces built by French behind village. Detached two men to supervise this. One case Enteric in 1/8 Bn. R. War Reg.	
12/9/15 "	To COUIN with A.D.M.S. - P.M. on 2 civilians horses - advised re burial & enclosure of area. Inspected billets at COIGNEUX	
13/9/15 "	Reinfector doing D.A.C. & THIEVRES. To COUIN re water, - and FONQUEVILLERS re refuse and latrines.	
14/9/15 "	Reinfector to Mob.Amb. Workshop for files at Bn.y platform. One case ? Enteric 1/8 R. Warwick Reg. F all End RAMC	

Forms/C. 2118/10

Army Form C. 2118.

WAR DIARY
or
INTELLIGENCE SUMMARY.
(Erase heading not required.)

Hour, Date, Place	Summary of Events and Information	Remarks and references to Appendices
15/10/15 BUS.	Routine. Disinfield downs 4th Warwick. On issue of flannel & surplus of cachet - issued to rounds & and total used on wed clothes after passage through disinfector.	
16/10/15 "	Routine. THIEVRES, FONQUEVILLERS, RAVENCOURT to AUTHIE.	
17/10/15 "	"	
18/10/15 "	to SAILLY re pulling out of founder of sick examined at MARIEUX - interviewed O.H. No.+ 4 Mob. Lab.	
19/10/15 "	LOUVENCOURT. One case ? Enteric in 5th Warwick.	
20/10/15 "	Disinfection doing 8th Warwick. To AUTHIE, GODIN SAILLY and COURCELLES. One case ? Typhoid in 5th Gloster.	
21/10/15 "	Disinfection doing 1/4th Worcester. One case civilian ? Typhoid in THIEVRES examined with O/C the 8th Mob.Lab. to AUTHIE re ? influenza in 4th Gloster. One case ? Enteric in 4th Oxfords.	
22/10/15 "	Disinfection doing 4th Gloster. To SOUILLENS, AUTHIE to PAS - int. O.C. Sandt 3rd/4th Div., to ACHEUX - O.C. 1st/4th R.W. One civilian typhoid diagnosed in SAILLY.	
23/10/15 "	Medical Board on outbreak in 4th Gloster's first diagnosed as ? Typhoid later Influenza - 61 cases in all - a mild febrile disorder - not diagnosed. Bacteriological examinations negative.
T. Dalcastrament	

WAR DIARY
or
INTELLIGENCE SUMMARY.
(Erase heading not required.)

Army Form C. 2118.

Hour, Date, Place	Summary of Events and Information	Remarks and references to Appendices
24 10/15 BUS	Routine. SAILLY, COURCELLES and ACHEUX. Case ? Typhoid in S.W. & Cyclists exam, with bacteriologist.	Sanitation of area generally improved – units more settled and more R.E. work done.
25 10/15 "	To Lt LEGER & AUTHIE re marking of wells.	Wells protected but not yet strictly satisfactory.
26 10/15 "	T. AUTHIE, BAYENCOURT, SAILLY.	Very important for the civilian population.
27 10/16 "	Disinfected buildgs in T.M.B + ?R. Worcesters, T. AUTHIE, MARIEUX, VAUCHELLES, LOUVENCOURT, DOULLENS.	Fly nuisance slightly. Latrine discipline generally good and trench sanitation very satisfactory
28 10/15 "	Disinfector with 1st F.A. B/de Amm. Col. To VAUCHELLES SAILLY + HEBUTERNE	Six cases of ?Enteric reptd from C.C.S. 2 and 3 of that confirmed.
29 10/16 "	Disinfector with 1st Sth. Fd Amb. To ARQUEVES.	Five cases of civilians typhoid in the ??confirmed Two in THIEVRES whose ?? have been about 12 cases since outbreak of war, and two in SAILLY where there is history of ?previous cases
30 10/16 "	One case mumps 5th Warwicks	

F. Dale Capt RAMC

Lice are a serious and increasing nuisance, some of the units which do not change billets much e.g. R.A., R.E. + Train manage to keep free but the whole of the infantry get more or less when clothes are thrilled with formalin & steam the men are soon lousy again. Brigadier Grand the men are ?? straw ?after a few days, to be burnt intelligently, ?? no ??prevented as yet but the sulphur is available presently.

Oct 19/15

S

19th Division
summarised but not copied
7449

49th Dn. Sanitary Secn.

Oct. 15

Vol VII

Confidential

War Diary

O.C. Sanitary Section, 48th (S.M.) Division
from
1st October 1915 to 31st October 1915.

(Volume y)

To The Officer,
i/c Adjutant-General's Office,
/SAC

Army Form C. 2118.

WAR DIARY
or
INTELLIGENCE SUMMARY.
(Erase heading not required.)

Instructions regarding War Diaries and Intelligence Summaries are contained in F.S. Regs., Part II. and the Staff Manual respectively. Title pages will be prepared in manuscript.

Hour, Date, Place	Summary of Events and Information	Remarks and references to Appendices
Oct 1st '15. BVS.	Section doing routine work — half of it detached as before in various villages and to R.O.H.Qt. To BAYENCOURT, LA HAIE and FONQUEVILLERS.	
2 $\frac{10}{15}$	2 cases ? Typhoid reported {1 in 6th Gordons {1 " 5th Warwicks. Routine. To BAYENCOURT. To O/c no 8 mobile lab re ? Typhoid in 5th Warwick. To DOULLENS re head re emphythium for sanitary purposes.	Re ? Typhoid cases in 5th Warwick. Attention was drawn to this on Oct 26/9 when No O/c seemed to enquiry that he had moved to evacuate & men in August and sent away 1 man in August & during September as ? Typhoid. 5 out of the 8 belonged to Staff Platoons of B. Coy., four of these had & been out from O/ttawa were reported ? Typhoid by Car clearing station. Two more cases were reported ? Typhoid by 8 CCS on Oct 4th, one coming from 5th
3 $\frac{10}{15}$	"	1 case ? Typhoid in 8th Warwick. " To FONQUEVILLERS. 1 case ? Typhoid in 5th Warwick
4 $\frac{10}{15}$	"	Disinfector with 4th Berks. To FOUASTRE. 2 cases ? Typhoid in 6th Warwick. 1 case ? " " 5th R.Lanc.
5 $\frac{10}{15}$	"	1 " Typhoid civilian in SAILLY. Disinfector still with 4th Berks. To FONQUEVILLERS re (1 ? typhoid cases in 5th Warwick).
6 $\frac{10}{15}$	"	3 civilian cases ? Typhoid notified in COIGNEUX. To COIGNEUX with bacteriologist re ? typhoid cases. To DOULLENS re hosp. accommodation for them and inoculation
7 $\frac{10}{15}$	"	To COIGNEUX re disinfectants. To SAILLY re removal of the case from there. Officially recommended inoculation of civilians in infected villages.
8 $\frac{10}{15}$	"	To COIGNEUX & SAILLY arranging inoculation of civilians & Motor Amb Workshop re making of water bowls from drains & CCS to COURCELLES.

In all 9 more or less definite cases were reported from 6th to week, which were isolated for some weeks. The stools of 9 convalescents and 3 acute cases were examined — all negative. 6 cases from the barracks at ? Typhoid by the C.C.S./Nov 3rd & 4th were confirmed by blood test as No fresh ? cases occurred after Oct 5th and no further ? has been Typhoid or the cause of the outbreak.

J. Kale Ref. Lt. R.M.S.

Form/C. 2118/10

Army Form C. 2118.

WAR DIARY
or
INTELLIGENCE SUMMARY.
(Erase heading not required.)

Hour, Date, Place		Summary of Events and Information	Remarks and references to Appendices
9 10/15	BUS.	Routine. With A.D.M.S. to all Fd Ambs. To COIGNEUX re inoct C to COIGNEUX again, inoculation begun. 49 full doses given to susceptibles (ages 6-45) 1 new ? case discovered there under care of civilian practitioner from adjoining area — refused to be examined by British.	
10 10/15	"	Routine. To DOULLENS & see Sub-prefect re refusal above detailed.	
11 10/15	"	" To AUTHIE & THIEVRES arranging inoculation. To LOUVENCOURT. Disinfector with 2d Fd Amb.	
12 10/15	"	" To COIGNEUX with Interp. Off & RADMS, also gendarme. ? case examined — very suspicious, still refuses to be moved. To AUTHIE once re inoculation — 53 susceptibles given full doses. Disinfector doing 8th Warwicks.	
13 10/15	"	" To COIGNEUX with interpreter & gendarme — ? case persuaded togo, and moved. To SAILLY re inoculation — being done by M.O. i/c Bn in billet. To THIEVRES inoculated 83 susceptibles. Disinfector with 4th Worcesters.	
14 10/15	"	Routine. Another ? Enteric civilian at SAILLY exam'd with backerishgat.	
15 10/15	"	Routine. To DOULLENS — Sub-prefect to write to Mayors recommending inoculation.	
16 10/15	"	Routine. To COURCELLES re inoculation — being done by M.O. i/c Bn in billet. To COIGNEUX & COUIN.	
17 10/15	"	Routine. With A.D.M.S. to BAVENCOURT-FONQUEVILLERS. To COIGNEUX — 13 first full doses and 35 second.	
18 10/15	"	Routine. Disinfector with 8th Worcesters. To COURCELLES, SAILLY COUIN & AUTHIE.	

F. Dale Capt. R.A.M.C.

WAR DIARY
or
INTELLIGENCE SUMMARY.
(Erase heading not required.)

Army Form C. 2118.

Instructions regarding War Diaries and Intelligence Summaries are contained in F.S. Regs., Part II. and the Staff Manual respectively. Title pages will be prepared in manuscript.

Hour, Date, Place	Summary of Events and Information	Remarks and references to Appendices
19 10/15 BUS	Routine. Disinfector with 1st Sia R.B. 86th R.F.A. ammcol. Willapus to THIEVRES. Visit of sub-prefect of DOULLENS + departmental delegate from Amiens re civilian typhoid outbreak. To AUTHIE inoculating civilians.	Civilian Typhoid in Area. During last winter + spring + early summer about 50 cases occurred chiefly along the valley of the R. Authie affecting the village of HEBUTERNE COIGNEUX (10 cases) AUTHIE (4 cases) THIEVRES (13 cases) FAMECHON (3rd Rv area—11 cases).
20 10/15 "	Routine. Disinfector with 2nd S.M. Fd. Amb. with ADMS to AUTHIE Inspected all billets. One ? typhoid civilian at AUTHIE (probably not typhd). To SAILLY.	Since Aug 1st at least 13 cases have been diagnosed as follows:— COURCELLES—1 case 40 inhabitants SAILLY—5 cases 250 inhabs—estimate COIGNEUX—5 cases—145 " Organisms THIEVRES—2 " 380 " by census made in Inspector
21 10/15 "	Routine. To AUTHIE and LOUVENCOURT.	These cases excl one who died under care of civilian drs have been
22 10/15 "	Routine. To COIN with ADMS inspected all billets to AUTHIE inoculating civilians.	diag- nosed with help of O.C. No 8 Mobile Lab and removed to French hospitals
23 10/15 "	Routine. O.C. No 9 Mob. Lab. examd D.W. drinking water supply at COIN to SAILLY.	at DOULLENS or AMIENS.
24 10/15 "	Routine. Visit of sub-prefect of DOULLENS re typhoid, inoculation, and provision of chlorinated water for civilians. To COIGNEUX inoculation. To HEBUTERNE with Sqd. S.O.2.	The necessary disinfections and placing out of bounds were carried out.
25 10/15 "	Routine. Disinfector with 64th Warwicks. To HEBUTERNE with civilians with water. To DOULLENS buying barrels to supply civilians with water.	Inoculation was offered to civil of all between ages of 6 + 45 being inoc'd a given a full dose and a second dose if they pass. Till later given.
26 10/15 "	Routine. Disinfector with 4th Berks. Inoculated at AUTHIE.	Up to date the following numbers have been done:— COURCELLES—14
27 10/15 "	Routine. Disinfector doing clothing from Baths. Men and fabrick destroyed of about 1 cubical capacity arrived.	SAILLY—90 = 60% (susceptible) COIGNEUX—91 = 90% " " AUTHIE—129 = 70% " " THIEVRES—112 = 66% " "
28 10/15 "	Routine. Bowel at ADMS office.	It will over 500 full doses have been given. Chlorinated water is being provided for civilians in villages affected French authorities have been consulted at all.
29 10/15 "	Routine. To BAYENCOURT. To THIEVRES + AUTHIE.	
30 10/15 "	Routine. To SAILLY + HEBUTERNE.	

J. Dale Capt R.A.M.C.

Army Form C. 2118.

WAR DIARY
or
INTELLIGENCE SUMMARY.
(Erase heading not required.)

Instructions regarding War Diaries and Intelligence Summaries are contained in F. S. Regs., Part II. and the Staff Manual respectively. Title pages will be prepared in manuscript.

Hour, Date, Place	Summary of Events and Information	Remarks and references to Appendices
31/10/15 BUS	Routine. To FONCQUEVILLERS. M.O. 4 & 9 Bat. campled well with one. To Coigneux inoculating.	Military typhoid in Area. Since Aug 1st at last 5 cases have been definitely featured amongst the troops of the 7th 2. Of these 3 were probably infected at SAILLY, 1 was possibly " " COIGNEUX the other was French infected. Stationed at FONCQUEVILLERS.
	T. Hale Capt RAMC	Sanitation of area fairly good - but it is very cold wet weather experienced during the month. Has made field sanitation difficult. Covered buckets latrines, ablution benches and cook houses are being provided everywhere by the R.E. - also drying rooms.
	The lice nuisance is as bad as ever. One great reason for this is the absence of any proper laundry arrangements If these can be made, and if petrolé treated bunks or at any rate palliasses can be provided for each man, and if a reasonable supply of Vermijelli and N.C.I. powder or their equivalents be obtained then the nuisance would be in my opinion greatly mitigated.	The bad weather has shown the discomfort of the billets. It is impossible to warm & light each billet but it is to be hoped that it will be possible to provide a sufficient number (properly warmed & lighted) recreation rooms in the various billeting centres. They are badly needed. Small stoves and a good supply of fuel are needed for the clergy. The French think - where the old men and women & boys are to think the women badly need.

Forms/C. 2118/10

Confidential
Summarised but not copied   121/7655

War Diary

of

O.C. Sanitary Section, 48th (S.M.) Division,

from 1st to 30th November 1915.

(Volume 8)

The Officer,
i/c Adjutant-General's Office,
Base.

Nov. '15
1st November 1915 to 30th November 1915.

WAR DIARY
or
INTELLIGENCE SUMMARY.
(Erase heading not required.)

Army Form C. 2118.

Hour, Date, Place	Summary of Events and Information	Remarks and references to Appendices
November 1 BUS.	Section doing routine work — 16 men detached in village in the area — acting under local M.O.'s. Conference with A.D.M.S., C.R.E., & D.A.Q.M.G. re sanitation — Latrines etc? To THIEVRES, MARIEUX, LOUVENCOURT & SAILLY. Disinfector in U.4 & Gloster at AUTHIE.	
2 " /15	Routine. Disinfector at BUS for 4/5 Warwicks. With R.A.M.S. to FONQUEVILLERS for 48 Warwicks and left trenches — satisfactory to AUTHIE inoculating civilians.	
3 " /15	Routine. Disinfector at yesterday. To BEAUVAL to see O.i/c No.8 Mot Lab.	
4 " /15	With R.D.M.S. to FONQUEVILLERS. To SAILLY. To COUIN — using camp for Bus attached for instruction.	
5 " /15	" To ST LEGER, SARTON, COUIN, FONQUEVILLERS with R.A.M.S. to AUTHIE inoculating. One case ? Typhoid — civilian at THIEVRES. One case ? Typhoid 1/1st Oxf & Bucks L.I.	
6 " /15	" To ST LEGER.	
7 " /15	" Visit of O.C. dau Dec 34th R.W. To THIEVRES. Two new Foden disinfectors improved types arrived — very useful — put out under charge of men attached. One case Enteric — Pte. J.H. Boe R.F.A. notified from base.	
8 " /15	" Disinfector at ST LEGER with 4/5 SMR & R.F.A. To ROSSIGNOL, BAYENCOURT, LA HAIE, THIEVRES & AUTHIE (Cap.H. Sho.) & COURCELLES.	
9 " /15	" Disinfector with 4/5 Oxf & Bucks at COURCELLES. The ? Typhoid civilian at THIEVRES refd — pos by Bacteriological & removed to AMIENS. To ARQUEVES, BEAUVAL, SAILLY-COURCELLES.	

V. Kale Capt R.A.M.C.

WAR DIARY
or
INTELLIGENCE SUMMARY.
(Erase heading not required.)

Army Form C. 2118.

Hour, Date, Place	Summary of Events and Information	Remarks and references to Appendices
10 11/15 BUS	Routine. Disinfector with 1st F. Amb at VAUCHELLES, ROSSIGNOL, & 2nd S.W. F.A. at LOUVENCOURT. Read paper to Med. Sec 5	
11 11/15 "	Routine. To THIEVRES — to see a civilian ? typhoid convalescent with army & civil or gcl — doubtful.	
12 11/15 "	To DOULLENS — interviewed sub-prefect To AUTHIE & LOUVENCOURT.	Civilian Typhoid in area.
13 11/15 "	O.C. on leave — T.A., R.M.S. doing duty. One civilian ? typhoid self from SAILLY	Two fresh cases have been diagnosed during the month. One at THIEVRES and one at SAILLY. Both removed to AMIENS.
21 11/15 "	One ? typhoid in 4th Berks Police.	Two other cases were discovered
22 11/15 "	Disinfector with 2nd S.W. F. Amb. at LOUVENCOURT. To ROSSIGNOL & BAYENCOURT.	to have occurred one in each of the above villages in July and August respectively, but
23 11/15 "	To SAILLY re ? S.F. To HEBUTERNE with R.A.M.S. — to centre trenches — falling in & sanitation of room pouring to bad weather. Disinfector with 4th Warwicks at BAYENCOURT	now well. Inoculation of inoculable civilians has proceeded
24 4/15 "	Disinfection yesterday. To ROSSIGNOL & COUIN.	slowly the percentage of inoculated being now about
25 11/15 "	To SAILLY — LA.HAIE & FONQUEVILLERS.	80% for all villages affected.
26 11/15 "	To COURCELLES. Case of ANTHRAX — 4th Berks Transport man.	
27 11/15 "	To SAILLY — the ? typhoid civilian reported to live went to AMIENS. Traced another case there missed in 1st report. To AUTHIE re the Anthrax case. To motor ambulance workshop who are making a new disinfector. J. Dale Capt. R.A.M.C.	Military Typhoid in area. One case has been definitely diagnosed during the month — probably infected in LONGNEUX.

WAR DIARY
or
INTELLIGENCE SUMMARY.

(Erase heading not required.)

Army Form C. 2118.

Hour, Date, Place	Summary of Events and Information	Remarks and references to Appendices
BUS. 28/11/15	Routine. To VAUCHELLES & LOUVENCOURT – interviewed German prisoner re lice etc.	Sanitation of area very difficult owing to the wet weather. Especially the latrine accommodation has been carried on underground with great difficulty. Covered deep bucket latrines were provided in most billeting centres. Incineration of refuse has proceeded very satisfactorily.
29/11/15	Routine. Disinfector broke down owing to frost. To VAUCHELLES – motor amb. workshop re same. Roads impassable.	The troops generally are very uncomfortable owing to the shortage of fuel, heating apt. water & lighting. The shortage of fuel is very serious – and hinders the washing and drying of clothing – use of improvised disinfectors etc. The lack of proper laundry facilities is also a cause of great discomfort.
30/11/15	" With S.A.D.M.S. to ARQUEVES, SAILLY, VAUTHIE, & DOULLENS and AUTHIEULE. F. Dale Capt. R.A.M.C. The lice nuisance seems rather less – probably owing to the use of small formalin steam disinfectors of which there are 8 in use as well as the Big Thresh machine. Unfortunately however it had not yet been possible enough to provide lack of material and offer lenses for most of the separate trunks or pullovers for most of the infantry – neither has any supply of preventive "Oxford" grease or powder yet been received. There have been a considerable number of scabies cases – the occurrence of which could probably be prevented if a sufficiency of lice preventives or sulphur could be obtained.	

"Confidential"
Summarised but not copied

War Diary
of
O.C. Sanitary Section, 48" (S.M.) Division.
from
1st December 1915 to 31st December 1915.

(Volume 9).

To The Officer,
i/c Adjutant-General's Office.
Base

Army Form C. 2118.

WAR DIARY
or
INTELLIGENCE SUMMARY.
(Erase heading not required.)

Hour, Date, Place	Summary of Events and Information	Remarks and references to Appendices
December		
1 12/15 BUS	Section doing routine work — 16 men detached in other villages throughout the area — acting under local M.O.t Trench disinfector — both 8 & Worcester at BUS. With A.D.M.S. to THIEVRES, VAUCHELLES, ARQUEVES & LOUVENCOURT. Routine. With D.A.D.M.G. to Supply Col.	
2 12/15	" To right sector trenches with D.D.M.S. — Trenches falling in — almost impossible to move, sanitation almost impossible.	
3 12/15	"	
4 12/15	" To AUTHIE and VAUCHELLES.	
5 12/15	" To BAYENCOURT. A case Cerebro-spinal meningitis 1/7 Bn R. War. Reg D?	
6 12/15	" To HEBUTERNE, SAILLY, THIEVRES, VAUCHELLES. Disinfector with 1st S.M. Fd Amb. at ARQUEVES.	
7 12/15	" To COUIN — civilian diphtheria there — 2/7 LEGER. To AUTHIE inoculating civilian. Disinfector with 2nd Fd Amb at LOUVENCOURT.	
8 12/15	" To COUIN & LOUVENCOURT. Disinfector at BAYENCOURT — 7/4 Warwicks.	
9 12/15	" With A.D.M.S. to FONCQUEVILLERS & BAYENCOURT.	
10 12/15	" To VAUCHELLES, AUTHIE & ARQUEVES.	
11 12/15	" To ARQUEVES & LOUVENCOURT.	

F. Dale Cmdr Maj. t.

WAR DIARY
or
INTELLIGENCE SUMMARY.
(Erase heading not required.)

Army Form C. 2118.

Instructions regarding War Diaries and Intelligence Summaries are contained in F. S. Regs., Part II. and the Staff Manual respectively. Title pages will be prepared in manuscript.

Hour, Date, Place	Summary of Events and Information	Remarks and references to Appendices
12 12/15 BUS	Routine. To COURCELLES.	
13 12/15 "	To AUTHEULE - Div. Luff Col. + VAUCHELLES. One case Cerebro-spinal meningitis in 4th Bn. Ox/+ Bks L.I. Disinfector at COURCELLES out.	
14 12/15 "	With R.A.M.S. to COURCELLES, SAILLY, BAYENCOURT and FONQUEVILLERS. Disinfector. BAYENCOURT - 8th Warwicks.	
15 12/15 "	With A.D.M.S. to COURCELLES, SAILLY, HEBUTERNE + BAYENCOURT. Disinfector with 8th Worcesters at BUS.	
16 12/15 "	With A.D.M.S. to SARTON, VAUCHELLES, ARQUÈVES.	
17 12/15 "	With Adj Gen + D.M.Q.M.G. to ST LEGER, AUTHIE, + five other villages in area. To AUTHIE inoculating civilians.	
18 12/15 "	W.A.D.M.S. to Field Ambulances and COURCELLES.	
19 12/15 "	With A.D.M.S. to ARQUÈVES and SARTON.	
20 12/15 "	To SAILLY + COUIN. One case ? typhoid reported in a civilian at THIÈVRES. Disinfector with 6th Gordons at COUIN.	The Thresh Foden lorry disinfector is henceforth attached to the Divn. 5 days per week instead of three. This very useful - especially for blankets. The small tox and improvised disinfectors could not deal with much clothing more or less infected. That the blanket badly needed precaution disinfection, from very twenty.
21 12/15 "	To AUTHIE. To THIÈVRES re ? typhoid above - already removed out of area - particulars forwarded to D.M.S. concerned. Disinfector to AUTHIE - 4th Gordons.	
22 12/15 "	To infector Bus-BUS - 5th Gordons.	F de la C + F. Rauch

WAR DIARY
or
INTELLIGENCE SUMMARY.
(Erase heading not required.)

Army Form C. 2118.

Hour, Date, Place	Summary of Events and Information	Remarks and references to Appendices
23 12/15 BUS.	Routine. With A.A.Q.M.G. and A.D.M.S. to AUTHIE, THIEVRES and Field Amb.. To COURCELLES re P.O.S. meningitic case in 4th Sx to R.R.L.I. To AUTHIEULE & DOULLENS. Disinfector at BUS - ref. to Transport.	Typhoid in area. No case has been diagnosed among civilians or troops during the month. The ? civilian case at THIEVRES was reported negative by the bacteriologist. Inoculation now frequently as complete as possible in the affected villages except at SAILLY where more volunteers should be raised.
24 12/15	To COURCELLES with Bacteriologist re ? meningitis above negative. Disinfector at COURCELLES with 4th Ox. & Bucks.	
25 12/15	With D.A.D.M.S. to SAILLY. With A.D.M.S. to HEBUTERNE and ROSSIGNOL.	Sanitation generally very difficult owing to the abnormal amount of rain - especially in the front line. Bucket latrines everywhere.
26 12/15	To SELEGER. Arranged Gallach man of section to Area Commander	
27 12/15	To AUTHIE inoculating civilians.	
28 12/15	To SAILLY & HEBUTERNE.— Disinfector at BAYENCOURT — 6th Warwicks	The Troops are well on the whole though some of the men are suffering worn out by the strain and discomfort. Almost all dugouts are now uninhabitable so that there is overcrowding in the other (?) function billets.
29 12/15	To BAYENCOURT. LA HAIE & FONQUEVILLERS. Disinfector as yesterday	
30 12/15	Disinfector at COURCELLES — 7th Worcester	
31 12/15	Disinfector at VAUCHELLES with 2/7th Reserve Park.	The weather has been warmer. The men complain greatly of the less from cold but the lack of fuel which still prevails gives rise to great discomfort by preventing washing of men and clothes, drying and disinfection of clothes. Scabies has diminished.

The lice nuisance is still bad though not as bad as it was. Washing and disinfection are hindered by lack of fuel and the majority of the infantry are still unprovided with separate drawers and pull-overs. Moreover there is shortage of straw so that even the common bedding sometimes cannot be changed. A supply of Oxford Greaser Powder has arrived and may be useful - but that cannot be expected to become of real while the above major disadvantages exist.

T. Dale Capt. R.A.M.C.

(Confidential).

War Diary
of
O.C. Sanitary Section, 48th (S.M.) Division
from
1st February 1916 to 29th February 1916.
(Volume XI).

To. The Officer,
   i/c. Adjutant-General's Office,

B.A.C.

WAR DIARY
or
INTELLIGENCE SUMMARY.
(Erase heading not required.)

Army Form C. 2118.

Hour, Date, Place	Summary of Events and Information	Remarks and references to Appendices
1 2/16 BUS	Section disposed as before — 13 men detached in outlying villages and with various Headquarters. Routine work — inspection and supervision of sanitary work, disinfection of laundry etc. One case Cerebro spinal meningitis 5th Bn R. Sussex Rgt.	
2 2/16 "	Routine. With A.D.M.S. to SAILLY, BAYENCOURT, & COUIN.	
3 2/16 "	" To LOUVENCOURT — arranging mending of clothes from Divisional Laundry.	
4 2/16 "	" Arranging for improvised disinfector to sterilise 600 suits of underclothing daily before despatch to PARIS and onwards. Foden lorry Thresh for other work.	
5 2/16 "	" To AMIENS with A.D.M.S. R.E. for parts for improvised disinfecting plant. To BERTRANCOURT.	
6 2/16 "	" To COURCELLES	
7 2/16 "	" Capt Thomason RAMC arrived to assist with Div Laundry scheme and take over supervision of same.	
8 2/16 "	"	
9 2/16 "	" To HEBUTERNE and SAILLY.	
10 2/16 "	" Improvised disinfector was completed, Foden Thresh now available for units — blankets etc.	
11 2/16 "	" To SAILLY.	

J. Poole Capt R.A.M.C.

Army Form C. 2118.

WAR DIARY
or
INTELLIGENCE SUMMARY.
(Erase heading not required.)

Instructions regarding War Diaries and Intelligence Summaries are contained in F. S. Regs., Part II. and the Staff Manual respectively. Title pages will be prepared in manuscript.

Hour, Date, Place	Summary of Events and Information	Remarks and references to Appendices
12 2/16 BUS.	Routine. Thresh Disinfector with 4th Div². To AUTHIE.	
13 2/16 "	"	
14 2/16 "	" To LOUVENCOURT.	
15 2/16 "	" Div² area extended to include SOUASTRE, RANNES CAMPS part of BIENVILLERS, BERTRANCOURT, COLINCAMPS and SARTON also trenches east of these villages. Village of LOUVENCOURT VAUCHELLES, ARQUÈVES, and COVIN no longer included in area. 12th Infantry B'de attached to Div².	
16 2/16 "	" To DOULLENS. Disinfector to 8th R. Warwicks. 1 case typhoid in 6th R'n Gloster.	
17 2/16 "	" To DOULLENS re payment of laundry in PARIS.	
18 2/16 "	"	
19 2/16 "	" To SOUASTRE. Arranged to detach man there to supervise sanitation.	
20 2/16 "	" One case German measles 4th Oxf⁰ Bucks L.I. To ST LEGER and AUTHIE. One case Cerebro-spinal meningitis.	
21 2/16 "	" To BERTRANCOURT with R.A.M.S. Disinfector with 4th Div². One case Cerebro-spinal meningitis 1/8th R. Warwicks.	
22 2/16 "	" " Paratyphoid " 1/8th R. Warwicks.	
23	" To SOUASTRE, FONQUEVILLERS, LA HAIE.	

V. Dale Capt R.A.M.C.

Army Form C. 2118.

WAR DIARY
or
INTELLIGENCE SUMMARY.
(Erase heading not required.)

Instructions regarding War Diaries and Intelligence Summaries are contained in F.S. Regs., Part II. and the Staff Manual respectively. Title pages will be prepared in manuscript.

Hour, Date, Place	Summary of Events and Information	Remarks and references to Appendices
BUS 2 3/5/16	Routine —	Sanitation of area fairly good; — That of the rear part taken over from 3 F.S.W. is being however open to strong objection; the latrines there were all of the trip or pan trench type with pot seat — only in winter and impossible in summer — also open to the objection that large masses of excreta are put deep into the earth where they may more easily contaminate civilian and perhaps military drinking water. Pail latrines were substituted as far as possible — the pail contents being disposed of in the usual fashion by use of the earth.
" 2 4/5/16	" O.C. on leave	
" 2 5/5/16	"	
" 2 6/5/16	" 1 case Cerebro-spinal meningitis Pte R.R. Warwick R.—.	
" 2 7/5/16	" 1 case German measles — Pte Sea Ranger Brown.	
" 2 8/5/16	"	
" 2 9/5/16	"	The health of the troops has been on the whole good except for a marked prevalence of bad coughs and colds. The weather except at the end of the month has been good.
	No cases of infectious disease have been reported among the civilian population; both of troops and civilians is still unfortunately held up by non-arrival of the new vaccine.	Infectious Disease One case of typhoid has been reported among the troops & that one paralytical. Miller (?). 4 cases of Cerebro-spinal meningitis have occurred — three in one Battalion
	Lice are less troublesome. The bathing facilities in the area are now very good, and the laundry scheme, by which the dirty clothes are disinfected and sent to PARIS daily for washing, is working satisfactorily. This disinfection is now done by an improved plant so that the last Foden Thresh and the smaller disinfectors are all available for units, which are also making more use of the Oxford grease and powder, especially of the latter. Scabies is still troublesome — fresh cases being continually introduced with drafts.	

T. Dale Capt. R.A.M.C. T.

(Confidential).

War Diary.

O.C. Sanitary Section, 48th (S.M.) Division,
from
1st March 1916 to 31st March 1916.
(Volume 12)

The Officer.
i/c. Adjutant-General's Office,
B A S E.

Army Form C. 2118.

WAR DIARY
or
INTELLIGENCE SUMMARY.
(Erase heading not required.)

Hour, Date, Place	Summary of Events and Information	Remarks and references to Appendices
BUS. 1 3/16	Section disposed as before — 12 men detached with Brigade Headquarters and advanced Dressing Stations in outlying village.	
" 2 3/16	Routine work — Inspection and supervision of sanitary work — disinfection of environs etc	
" 3 3/16	Routine. O.C. on leave. R.A.M.C. i/c of section.	
" 4 3/16	"	
" 5 3/16	"	
" 6 3/16	12th Inf. Bde leaves Div. Same evacuated by Bus. — also BERTRANCOURT. O.C. returned from leave. To COURCELLES with R.A.M.S.	
" 7 3/16	Lieut Hill R.A.M.C., O.C. Sanitects 35th Div attached for instruction. To COURCELLES and COLINCAMPS. Two cases German Measles.	
" 8 3/16	To SAILLY & HEBUTERNE.	
" 9 3/16	To SOUASTRE & COIGNEUX.	
" 10 3/16	O.C. Influenza.	
" 11 3/16	1 case German measles.	
" 12 3/16	To FONQUEVILLERS.	
" 13 3/16	To BAYENCOURT, SOUASTRE & COUIN. Two cases German Measles.	
" 14 3/16	To COURCELLES, COLINCAMPS, the SUCRERIE. Two cases German Measles	
" 15 3/16	To ARQUÈVES. One case German Measles	

Dale Capt. R.A.M.C.

Army Form C. 2118.

WAR DIARY
or
INTELLIGENCE SUMMARY.
(Erase heading not required.)

Instructions regarding War Diaries and Intelligence Summaries are contained in F. S. Regs., Part II. and the Staff Manual respectively. Title pages will be prepared in manuscript.

Hour, Date, Place		Summary of Events and Information	Remarks and references to Appendices
BUS	16 3/16	Routine. O.C. sick	
"	17 3/16	"	
"	18 3/16	" One case Paratyphoid B — 1/4 TR Rankl.	
"	19 3/16	" Lieut HILL, RAMC returned to S.S. of WH. Foden-Truck disinfector to 36 D.W.	
"	20 3/16	" To COVIN re removal thither of Div H.Qrs	
"	21 3/16	"	
"	22 3/16	" Disinfector returned to Bus.	
"	23 3/16	" To COVIN. Six cases German measles	
"	24 3/16	" One case German measles	
"	25 3/16	" To COVIN.	
"	26 3/16	" BUS evacuated. H.Q.Qrs and details move to COVIN	
COVIN	27 3/16	" 7 cases German measles	
"	28 3/16	" With R.A.M.S. to HEBUTERNE & SAILLY Three cases German measles, 1 case cerebro-spinal fever in 1/5 7th Bn Gloster.	
"	29 3/16	" To SOUASTRE. six cases German measles	
"	30 3/16	" To AILLY, COLINCAMPS, COURCELLES and trenches of right sector Three cases German measles.	
"	31 3/16	" To ST. LEGER.	

Sheale Capt. R.A.M.C.

Army Form C. 2118.

WAR DIARY
or
INTELLIGENCE SUMMARY.
(Erase heading not required.)

Hour, Date, Place	Summary of Events and Information	Remarks and references to Appendices
March 1916 BVS	Sanitation of area fairly satisfactory. Health of the troops less satisfactory — they are very stale and the weather has been very trying. Numerous cases of influenza ("trenchfever") and coughs and colds. Infectious Disease. An outbreak of German measles — 37 cases diagnosed and sent away — affecting chiefly the two Bns. in each of two bgs. (Bde). It is in my opinion too late to avoid the trouble — even if it is possible — to take effective steps to check this disease. Many cases are so mild coverage that they are missed, and the patient is as a rule not incapacitated for more than a day or two, if at all. A number of the cases were drafts who developed the disease within a day or two of arrival. One case of Enteric (Para B) was reported. He had left the Div. 6 weeks previously with flu uring. It is remarkable that of 5 cases of Para B notified from Base during the last 12 months — in 4 cases a period of 6 weeks elapsed between departure of patient and notification. During 12 months 13 Typhoid; 5 Para B; 1 Para A have been definitely diagnosed. 13 cases of Cerebro-spinal Fever " " There has been no case of infectious disease reported among the civilians during march. Lice are still very generally present but not troublesome — probably owing to satisfactory bath and laundry scheme. Scabies is greatly diminished. It is said that a considerable proportion of the patients are infected worst in the region of the buttocks — ? latrine seats. Fale Capt RAMC	

(Confidential)

War Diary

O.C. Sanitary Section, 48th (S.M.) Division,
from 1st April 1916 to 30th April 1916.
(Volume 13)

To The Officer,
i/c Adjutant-General's Office,
BASE.

Army Form C. 2118.

WAR DIARY
or
INTELLIGENCE SUMMARY.
(Erase heading not required.)

Instructions regarding War Diaries and Intelligence Summaries are contained in F. S. Regs., Part II. and the Staff Manual respectively. Title pages will be prepared in manuscript.

Hour, Date, Place	Summary of Events and Information	Remarks and references to Appendices
COUIN 1/7/16	Section disposed as before - 14 men detached with Brigade Headquarters, Advd Dressing Stn, and Town Major of village.	
" 2/7/16	Routine work - inspection, supervision of sanitary work, disinfection etc.	
" 3/7/16	O.C. inoculated. 3 cases German measles.	
" 4/7/16	Routine. 1 case G. measles.	
" 5/7/16	" Conference of M.O.s at A.D.M.S' Office. 2 cases G. measles.	
" 6/7/16	"	
" 7/7/16	" To AMIENS ref Laundry etc. 2 cases G. measles.	
" 8/7/16	" To AUTHIE.	
" 9/4/16	" Visit of R.A.M.C. officer of 31st Divn to see improvised disinfector. Arro of O.C. 2nd Lectr ?1 R.D.W.	
" 10/7/16	" With A.D.M.S. to FONQUEVILLERS, SOUASTRE.	
" 11/7/16	" To SAILLY & BAYENCOURT. 2 cases G. measles.	
" 12/7/16	" With A.D.M.S. & A.A.Q.M.G. to HEBUTERNE & SAILLY. 3 cases G. measles.	
" 13/7/16	" 5 cases G. measles.	
" 14/7/16	" To ROSSIGNOL. Lecture to Divl School on inoculation	
" 15/7/16	" To ST LEGER & AUTHIE. 5 cases G. measles.	

F. Cole Capt R.A.M.C.

Army Form C. 2118.

WAR DIARY
or
INTELLIGENCE SUMMARY.
(Erase heading not required.)

Instructions regarding War Diaries and Intelligence Summaries are contained in F. S. Regs., Part II. and the Staff Manual respectively. Title pages will be prepared in manuscript.

Hour, Date, Place	Summary of Events and Information	Remarks and references to Appendices
COUIN 14/4/16	ROUTINE. Rules for reconstitution of Returned draft & forwarded.	Copy marked (A.)
" 15/4/16	" 4 cases G. Measles	
" 16/4/16	" To COIGNEUX. re attachment of men to Town Mayor — Arranged.	
" 17/4/16	" 1 case G. Measles. 1 case Typhoid in 4th Bn Oxf & Buck L.I.	
" 18/4/16	" To SOUASTRE, FONQUEVILLERS, LA HAIE, BAYENCOURT & HÉBUTERNE 1 case G. Measles.	
" 19/4/16	" To THIÈVRES & AUTHIE — inspection of river & of RW STRAIN.	
" 20/4/16	" To THIÈVRES & FAMECHON — inspection of River QUILIENNE. Report to A.D.M.S. on bad condition of RW Waterearts. 2 cases German Measles.	
" 21/4/16	" To BAYENCOURT, SAILLY & COIGNEUX.	
" 22/4/16	" With A.P.M. inspecting rivers to COIGNEUX. 2 cases G. Measles.	
" 23/4/16	" To ST LEGER & AUTHIE completing inspection of R. AUTHIE 3 cases G. measles.	
" 24/4/16	" O.C. on special leave 7 days. 4 cases G. measles.	
" 25/4/16	" Foden-Thresh disinfector henceforth to go to other DW 21 4 days per week instead of two.	
" 26/4/16	" 2 cases G. Measles	

Hale Capt RAMC

Army Form C. 2118.

WAR DIARY
or
INTELLIGENCE SUMMARY.
(Erase heading not required.)

Instructions regarding War Diaries and Intelligence Summaries are contained in F.S. Regs., Part II. and the Staff Manual respectively. Title pages will be prepared in manuscript.

Hour, Date, Place	Summary of Events and Information	Remarks and references to Appendices
COCIN. 27/4/16	Routine. O.C. on special leave. 6 cases G. measles.	
" 28/4/16	" 1 case G. measles.	
" 29/4/16	" 1 " " "	
" 30/4/16	" 3 " " "	

F. Dale Capt. R.A.M.C.T.

Sanitation of area fairly good. In the village of WIZERNES where there was an exceptional lack of civilian latrine accommodation an Ordre has been issued by the Mayor enforcing the provision of the same. It has proved useful. Similar ones can be issued elsewhere. A copy is attached marked (B.)

Health of the troops fair. A good deal of minor sickness including 3 cases of German measles diagnosed.

One case of typhoid among the troops - the patient was only one month with the B.E.F. 2 weeks sick - and was reported from the Base 4 weeks later.

No serious disease reported among civilians

Lice still prevalent but not troublesome - plenty of baths and clean underclothes.

F. Dale Capt R.A.M.C.T.

Forms/C. 2118/10

(A)

Copy

A.D.M.S. 48th Divn

I beg to suggest that Town Majors be advised that troops be only allowed to use Estaminets which carry out the following regulations:-

(1) The Latrine used by the owner must be kept clean. It must be either a hole in the ground or a bucket latrine, and the excreta must be always covered with dry earth or ashes. No other form of Latrine may be used.

(2) A screened urinal must be provided in a conspicuous position for the guests to the Estaminet. Oil drums or petrol tins should be used as vessels and should be emptied daily into a covered pit. The floor of the urinal should be kept dry.

(3) Refuse bins should be provided and the contents disposed of daily as the Town Major may direct.

(4) Premises to be kept clean; all manure to be regularly removed.

(5) All water served to troops or used for washing glasses to be boiled or chlorinated.

J. Dale Capt. R.A.M.C.T.
Divisional Sanitary Officer, 48th Divn

11/4/16

Translated into French & distributed by A.P.M. to Estaminet keepers. Town Majors notified and requested to report non compliance to A.P.M.

(B)

Préfecture de la Somme.   Copy

Canton d'Acheux.   Commune de St-Léger-les-Authies.
                        Département de la Somme.

Arrêté Municipal.

Nous, Maire de la Commune,
Vu la loi municipale du 5 Avril, 1884,
Vu la loi du 15 Février 1902,
Vu le nombre insuffisant des lieux d'aisances dans le village
Vu le danger qui peut résulter du transport par les mouches des germes microbiens contenus dans les matières fécales, aussi bien que de la souillure des eaux par les dites matières,

Arrêtons :

Article premier :- Tout dépôt de matières fécales en quelque quantité que ce soit, à la surface des voies publiques, sentiers, cours, ou terrains vagues, est interdit dans toute l'étendue de la partie habitée de la commune;

Article 2 : Les personnes n'ayant pas de lieux d'aisances devront creuser une fosse profonde d'au moins 0m.60 et à une distance minimum de 20 mètres de leur habitation. Cette fosse sera fréquemment désinfectée par la chaux, le chlore ou le crésyl, elle sera recouverte de terre et une nouvelle fosse sera creusée chaque fois qu'il sera nécessaire.

Article 3 :- Chaque matin, chacun devra déposer devant son habitation et sur la route, tous les détritus du ménage rendus inutilisables : épluchures, cendres, etc...
Une voiture militaire passera chaque jour vers neuf heures pour enlever ces ordures ménagères.

Article 4 : Le fumier devra séjourner le moins longtemps possible dans les cours. Il sera enlevé et transporté aux champs au moins une fois par semaine.

Article 5 :- Les contraventions aux dispositions du présent arrêté seront poursuivies conformément à l'article 27 de la loi du 15 Février 1902.

Fait à St-Léger-les-Authies, le 1er avril, 1916,
                                    Le Maire.

(Confidential)

War Diary.
of
Sanitary Section. 48th (Sm) Division

from

1st May 1916 to 31st May 1916.

(Volume 14)

Army Form C. 2118.

WAR DIARY
or
INTELLIGENCE SUMMARY.
(Erase heading not required.)

Instructions regarding War Diaries and Intelligence Summaries are contained in F.S. Regs., Part II. and the Staff Manual respectively. Title pages will be prepared in manuscript.

Hour, Date, Place	Summary of Events and Information	Remarks and references to Appendices
COUIN 1 5/16	Routine work — 12 men detached with R.C. H.Q. at Town major, and one to R.E. station. Rest of section at Disinfecting station and Head Quarters.	
" 2 5/16	O.C. on leave. R.A.D.M.S. 4/a	
" 3 5/16	Routine. O.C. on leave.	
" 4 5/16	" O.C. sick in S.M.C.C.S.	
" 5 5/16	Div^l area reduced. FONQUEVILLERS, SOUASTRE BAYENCOURT, + part of SAILLY + HEBUTERNE evacuated. 144 F.R&E to BEAUVAL.	
" 6 5/16	O.C. returned to duty.	
" 7 5/16	" To SAILLY + COURCELLES.	
" 8 5/16	"	
" 9 5/16	" With A.D.M.S. to BEAUVAL, GEZAINCOURT, HEM — the new rest billet area.	
" 10 5/16	" To BUS, AUTHIE, ST. LEGER.	
" 11 5/16	" With D.A.D.M.S. to trenches V + G. sections — sanitation fairly good. HEBUTERNE. Lecture to Pinte School.	
" 12 5/16	"	
" 13 5/16	" To MARIEUX, to see left flank at Corps Hd. Qrs. to BEAUQUESNE disinfection for Corps to BEAUVAL + GEZAINCOURT arranged to attach men to town majors there.	
" 14 5/16	"	Dale Capt R.A.M.C.

Army Form C. 2118.

WAR DIARY
or
INTELLIGENCE SUMMARY.
(Erase heading not required.)

Hour, Date, Place		Summary of Events and Information	Remarks and references to Appendices
COUIN	15 5/16	Routine. COUIN & ST LEGER – men attached to Town Major	
"	16 5/16	" W.A.A.D.S.S., to ST LEGER. To COIGNEUX.	
"	17 6/16	" To COIGNEUX and ST LEGER	
"	18 5/16	" To BEAUVAL & GEZAINCOURT.	
"	19 5/16	" To SAILLY & COIGNEUX	
"	20 5/16	" To ST LEGER & AUTHIE. One case ? typhoid civilian in COUIN.	
"	21 5/16	"	
"	22 5/16	" Visit of O.C. Sanitary Section 57th Div.	
"	23 6/16	" To COIGNEUX, HEBUTERNE, Trenches &c, re chlor. lecture to Div. School. Above mentioned ? typhoid refuses to see O.C. Mob. Bact. Lab. pending that civilian Dr. says it is influenza. French medical officer from ACHEUX to see ? typhoid – Case removed to AMIENS.	
"	24 5/16	" To FAMECHON & PAS re hosp. tour of RIQUILIENNE by 57th Div. Baths.	
"	25 5/16	" one case paratyphoid B. in 4th R. Berks.	
"	26 5/16	" Visit of Sanitary Offr. 4th Army. First time in 14 months that Div has been visited by sanitary offr in superior position (?) man detached to Town Major SAILLY.	
"	27 5/16	" To COIGNEUX & AUTHIE.	
"	28 5/16	" To ROSSIGNOL, SAILLY & HEBUTERNE with C.R.E. One ? typhoid 46th Res. Park.	
"	29 5/16	" W.A. R.A.M.S. Corps to ST LEGER & AUTHIE.	

Army Form C. 2118.

WAR DIARY
or
INTELLIGENCE SUMMARY.
(Erase heading not required.)

Hour, Date, Place	Summary of Events and Information	Remarks and references to Appendices
30 5/16 COUIN	Routine. Conference at Corps H Q. re of O.C. & Sen Section of Amb with Sanitary Off. Army. To SAILLY-au-HERLEVNE.	
31 5/16 COUIN	" To AUTHIE, & FAMECHON. K.A.M.S. on leave OC. to visit A.D.M.S.	
	Hale Capt R.A.M.C.	
	Sanitation of area fair. In the villages in the Authie valley occupied all winter by artillery horse lines — there has been a good deal of untidiness and there is a great deal of mud and manure to be moved. It is very difficult to get labour for this, though a few P.B. men have recently been attached to the Div's who will be of some use in this connection. It is very difficult to get carts for moving up manure etc and impossible at this time to get civilian carts.
Health of troops fair — a good deal of influenza, (German trenches) (diminishing) and scabies.
One case of Paratyphoid B. among the troops and one ?Typhoid civilian infection not traced in either case.
Lice not troublesome. The pulling of anti lice ointment — soft soap & paraffin — about the dressing rooms of the Batts will notices telling the men to use it was found to be a means of getting ointment used without waste. at the moment it is however impossible to get soft soap from Ordnance.	
	Hale Capt R.A.M.C.	

Confidential
War Diary
of
O.C. Sanitary Section 48th (S.M.) Divn.

from

1st June 1916 to 30th June 1916.

Volume 15.

Army Form C. 2118.

WAR DIARY
or
INTELLIGENCE SUMMARY.
(Erase heading not required.)

Instructions regarding War Diaries and Intelligence Summaries are contained in F. S. Regs., Part II. and the Staff Manual respectively. Title pages will be prepared in manuscript.

Place	Date	Hour	Summary of Events and Information	Remarks and references to Appendices
COUIN	1/6/16		Routine work — varying number of men detached with Inf. Bde, Town Majors, and Adv. Dressing Stns — remainder at Headquarters.	
"	2/6/16		Routine. Inspection in COUIN and ST LEGER	
"	3/6/16		Routine. To AUTHIE.	
"	4/6/16	"	To ST LEGER and AUTHIE. Two Inf. Bdes evacuate BEAUVAL area and go near ABBEVILLE for training.	
"	5/6/16	"	AUTHIE evacuated by Div. To HEBUTERNE with ADMS. & Adjt. R.E.	
"	6/6/16	"	To Training area — visited Bdes there, also Supply Col's at FIENVILLERS.	
"	7/6/16	"	To COIGNEUX	
"	8/6/16	"	To SAILLY, LITTLE DELL & COIGNEUX.	
"	9/6/16	"	To ST LEGER	
"	10/6/16	"	To COIGNEUX.	
"	11/6/16	"	To HEBUTERNE and trenches with R.A.M.C.	
"	12/6/16	"	To SAILLY & COIGNEUX. Inf. Bdes return from training area to hut'g bivouac at COUIN, COIGNEUX & SAILLY (Dell)	
"	13/6/16	"	To COIGNEUX. Memorandum & sketch of fly proof latrines sent out.	marked A.
"	14/6/16	"	To HEBUTERNE & SAILLY. One ? Typhoid & 17th Siege B.ty R.G.A — unit visited.	
"	15/6/16	"	Lecture to RWF School on Sanitation.	

Steele Capt. R.A.M.C.
D.A.D.S.

Army Form C. 2118.

WAR DIARY
or
INTELLIGENCE SUMMARY.
(Erase heading not required.)

Instructions regarding War Diaries and Intelligence Summaries are contained in F. S. Regs., Part II. and the Staff Manual respectively. Title pages will be prepared in manuscript.

Place	Date	Hour	Summary of Events and Information	Remarks and references to Appendices
COVIN	16/6/16		Routine. To SAILLY "the DELL"	
"	17/6/16		To SAILLY with A.D. Took over charge of Baths & Laundry from Capt Thomson. Left Fitzpatrick evacuated sick. Pte Price of 61st S.M. Div't Sanitary Section arrived as reinforcement for 2nd Sn. Fd Amb. — taken on strength of same section	
"	18/6/16		To SAILLY re proximity of latrines to new wells	
"	19/6/16		To Trenches H. sector — very clean. several Pyrexia from 74th Siege B.B. two with large Spleen. Bacteriologist wired for	
"	20/6/16		To SAILLY.	
"	21/6/16		To COIGNEUX & SAILLY. Testing & pcl water supplies with Horrocks apparatus. 1/4 measure required at main supplies at COVIN COIGNEUX & SAILLY (Well) 2 men of section placed on duty at each source to supervise chlorination — relieving Fd Amb. men now withdrawn.	
"	22/6/16			
"	23/6/16		To ST LEGER.	
"	24/6/16		To COIGNEUX. Bombardment begins on this front.	
"	25/6/16		To SAILLY. Interviewed new M.O. 4th Gordons.	
"	26/6/16			
"	27/6/16		To MAILLY — Pommier ridge with MASH's.	
"	28/6/16		Clearing up — in preparation for move	

F. Dale Capt RAMC
O/C

Army Form C. 2118.

WAR DIARY
or
INTELLIGENCE SUMMARY.
(Erase heading not required.)

Instructions regarding War Diaries and Intelligence Summaries are contained in F. S. Regs., Part II. and the Staff Manual respectively. Title pages will be prepared in manuscript.

Place	Date	Hour	Summary of Events and Information	Remarks and references to Appendices
COUIN	29/7		Routine work to SAILLY. 1 case Diphtheria & several suspects in 4th Berks at COUIN. Baths & Laundry 'closed down' pending of perlum.	
"	30/7		Routine. Sanitation of the greatly reduced area has been fair — though the impossibility of obtaining or hiring labour and carts under the stress of circumstances has practically limited all work to 'current' military sanitation. It has not been possible to move civilian manure etc. Fortunes & burrows to the extent met with — flies are still very few. Military manure has been quickly & nearly all latrines have been made fly-proof — with deepest of forces by incineration near water supplies and deep trenches when clear of same. Health of troops good. German measles has ceased & scabies is less. One case of Paratyphoid A reported from Base & not yet traced. Lice not troublesome but still generally prevalent. Baths Laundry & disinfector stated working well.	

Hale Capt RAMC
O/c

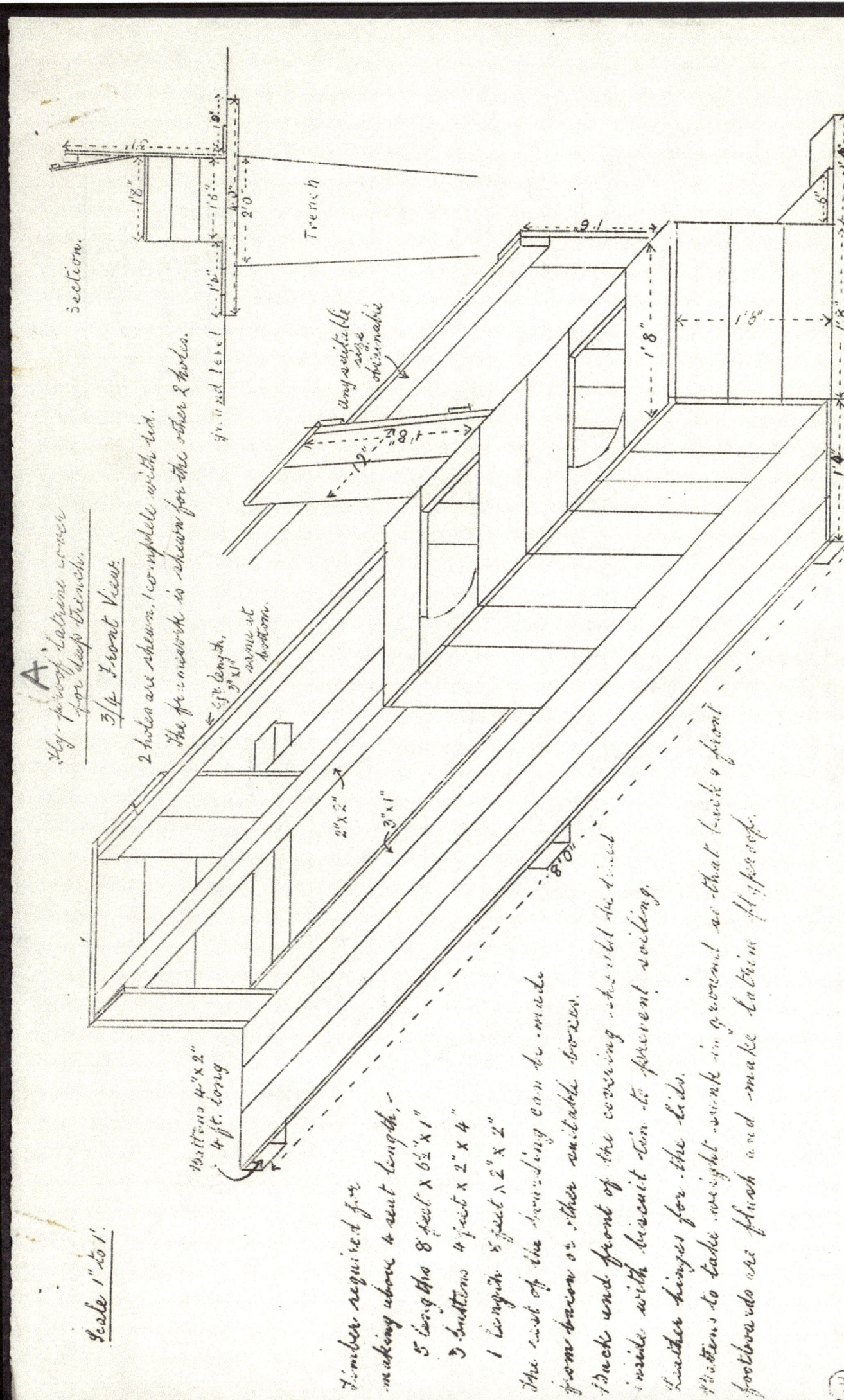

(Confidential)

War Diary

of

O.C. Sanitary Section - 48th (S.M.) Divn:

from

1st July 1916 to 31st July 1916.

(Volumn 16)

Army Form C. 2118.

WAR DIARY
or
INTELLIGENCE SUMMARY
(Erase heading not required.)

Instructions regarding War Diaries and Intelligence Summaries are contained in F.S. Regs., Part II. and the Staff Manual respectively. Title Pages will be prepared in manuscript.

Place	Date	Hour	Summary of Events and Information	Remarks and references to Appendices
COUIN	1/7/16		Section disposed as before — 14 men detached with 18th Bde Hd. Qrs, Town Majors, and Ass't Brig Stations; remainder of section at H Qs. Quarters COUIN. Routine work — supervising and inspecting work, sanitary work, disinfection of clothing for laundry, management of baths. Heavy fighting on front. O.C. 2 Lieut and lorry went at various dressing stations. 10 men with 2 N.C. Hd. Qrs and 2 half Bdgs to MAILLY-MAILLET. O.C. & A. Dm's office COUIN as yesterday.	
"	2/7/16		Hd Qr and Bdgs return to COUIN area. O.C. to SAILLY. Trenches in COLINCAMPS sector taken over from 31st Divn.	
"	3/7/16			
"	4/7/16		Routine work. Visited COLINCAMPS sector of trenches. Sanitation almost nil and conditions exceedingly difficult. Sent up partly to night to carry creosol, drums, etc — P/S FENN wounded by shrapnel in right foot to hospital.	
"	5/7/16			
"	6/7/16		Routine. Visited HEBUTERNE trenches not very bad.	
"	7/7/16		Routine. Examined main water supplies for very heavy rain of yesterday. Quality apparently unaltered	
"	8/7/16		To ST LEGER.	
"	9/7/16		To COLINCAMPS trenches — improving but heavily shelled; AUTHIE infected.	
"	10/7/16		To DOULLENS for material. AUTHIE infected.	
"	11/7/16		To SAILLY & COURCELLES. Temporary water tanks at COURCELLES very dirty — fault of action.?	
"	12/7/16		To COLINCAMPS, COURCELLES, & COIGNEUX — Town major.	
"	13/7/16		Lecture to B.W. School.	

Dudley Cork Capt. R.A.M.C.

Army Form C. 2118.

WAR DIARY
or
INTELLIGENCE SUMMARY

(Erase heading not required.)

Instructions regarding War Diaries and Intelligence Summaries are contained in F. S. Regs., Part II. and the Staff Manual respectively. Title Pages will be prepared in manuscript.

Place	Date	Hour	Summary of Events and Information	Remarks and references to Appendices
COUIN	14/7/16		Routine. To SAILLY & COURCELLES.	
"	15/7/16		Preparing to move. Handing over to O.C. Sanit Sect 3 85 Div. Detached men called in except those with Bde.	
"	16/7/16		Move to BOUZINCOURT. Village and area exceedingly dirty. Flies very prevalent – for the first time this year.	
BOUZINCOURT	17/7/16		Routine. Visited SENLIS – 10th CORPS Hd Qrs v. dirty. Attached 2 men to Town Major.	
"	18/7/16		Arranged baths in BOUZINCOURT. Sent. off fire at Corps H.Q.	
"	19/7/16		Visited Bde H.Qrs in line and LA BOISELLE. Detached 1 NCO to Corps Hd Qrs and 2 extra men to each of the two Bdes in the line.	
"	20/7/16		To 143 & 145 Bde H.Q. in line and LA BOISELLE re water. To AVELUY – attached N.C.O. to Town Major.	
"	21/7/16		To 144 Bde & two Bns in line in OVILLERS.	
"	22/7/16		To COUIN with lorry for clothes and stores. Lorry at night to Cent. Dy 9th Ek ALBERT for sitting cases.	
"	23/7/16		To SENLIS – Town Major and AVELUY re water – mains sufficient.	
"	24/7/16		Testing water from German well in OVILLERS – no poisons!	
"	25/7/16		To AMIENS – with lorry to laundry for clothes.	
"	26/7/16		To AVELUY and the 3 Bde Hd Qr in line.	
"	27/7/16		Preparing to move. Handing over to OC Sani Section 12 Div. Detached men recalled except to men with Bde Hd Qrs.	
"	28/7/16		Move to LE PLOUY. Area apparently clean, not recently occupied by troops. Flies prevalent from civilian farmers.	

Date Capt R.A.M.C.T

WAR DIARY or INTELLIGENCE SUMMARY

Army Form C. 2118.

Place	Date	Hour	Summary of Events and Information	Remarks and references to Appendices
LE PLOUY	29/7/16		Routine. Arranging baths in BONQUEUR - fixing extemporised disinfector for clothing from baths. Foden lorry to D.O.R.S. left at BOUZINCOURT with 12th N.F.	
"	30/7/16		Routine. To BONQUEUR & supply cols at VIGNACOURT for material for baths.	
"	31/7/16		Routine. To DOULLENS for RE material for disinfectors.

A sanitation in the area immediately behind the line where fighting is going on is exceedingly difficult owing to constant changes of troops in occupation. It rests apt in the appointment of our own major & area commanders as far as possible and the placing under them orders of working parties who are not frequently changed. This is beginning to some extent.

The tendency of the Division before to be limited during these moves to the proper disposal of excreta - especially its protection from flies, the prohibition of food from flies, which is much more difficult, and the supervision of water supplies. It is not possible to satisfactorily dispose of horse manure, though a certain amount is burned. The incinerary refuse of the troops is burned.

The only cases of infectious disease reported during the month were one case enteric group, one case Paratyphoid A and one Paratyphoid B.

There has been a considerable amount of Influenza or Trench fever - and the troops are now very lousy again - for which it is not possible to do much under present conditions. N.C.I. powder had a good ointment are still unprocurable. | |

Dale Capt R.A.M.C.

Vol 17

(Confidential)
War Diary
of
O.C. Sanitary Section 48th (S.M.) Div:
from
1st August 1916 to 31st August 1916.
(Volumn 17)

COMMITTEE FOR THE
MEDICAL HISTORY OF THE WAR
Date -5 OCT.1916

WAR DIARY
INTELLIGENCE SUMMARY

Army Form C. 2118.

Place	Date	Hour	Summary of Events and Information	Remarks and references to Appendices
LE PLOUY	1 8/16		Div¹ at rest — 8 men detached with B⁰⁶⁵ Corps & Army Hd. Qrs — Routine work — inspection and supervision of sanitary work, disinfection of clothing, management of baths. O.C. 6 MAISON ROLLAND.	
"	2 8/16		Routine. With Sections. To SURCAMPS, FRANQUEVILLE & FRANZU — B¹¹ in billets	
"	3 8/16		" To ST OUEN — Camp of R.A.	
"	4 8/16		" To MESNIL DOMQUEUR, COULONVILLERS — B¹¹ in billets	
"	5 8/16		" To AMIENS — searching for laundries — visited 5 frustless	
"	6 8/16		" New Foden-Thresh arrived disinfection begun at bath DOMQUEUR	
"	7 8/16		" To AMIENS re laundries.	
"	8 8/16		" To AMIENS & BOVES re laundries	
"	9 8/16		Div¹¹ moves to BEAUVAL area. To BOUZINCOURT & SENLIS — visited D.D.M.S. 12ᵗʰ Div¹¹	
BEAUVAL	10 8/16		Routine. To LE PLOUY & DOMQUEUR where 6 men & FODEN-THRESH remained disinfecting clothing from baths. O.C. ran section 12ᵗʰ Div¹¹	
"	11 8/16		To LE PLOUY — closing baths & disinfecting station. Foden Thresh returned to 1ˢᵗ Corps.	
"	12 8/16		Routine. To AMIENS to take over Laundry at SALEUX from 12ᵗʰ Div¹¹.	
"	13 8/16		MOVE to BOUZINCOURT. Div¹¹ in line. Took over from O.C. San Sec 12ᵗʰ Div¹¹	
BOUZINCOURT	14 8/16		Routine. To AMIENS — SALEUX Laundry. Baths at BOUZINCOURT, Foden Thresh disinfector arrived for the Div¹¹.	
"	15		Routine. To OVILLERS — regimental aid posts of B¹¹ in line.	

Hbale Capt R.A.M.C.

WAR DIARY
or
INTELLIGENCE SUMMARY
(Erase heading not required.)

Army Form C. 2118.

Instructions regarding War Diaries and Intelligence Summaries are contained in F. S. Regs, Part II. and the Staff Manual respectively. Title Pages will be prepared in manuscript.

Place	Date	Hour	Summary of Events and Information	Remarks and references to Appendices
BOUZINCOURT	16/8/16		Routine. To SALEUX laundry.	
"	17/8/16		" To ALBERT re BOUZINCOURT water supply which varies greatly in quality. One man detached to Advd. H.Q. at Crucifix Corner.	
"	18/8/16		" To AMIENS re Canteen.	
"	19/8/16		" To AMIENS – pay day at laundry.	
"	20/8/16		" To OVILLERS re water supply.	
"	21/8/16		" To AVELUY Town Major & O.C. R.E. Coy dealing with water. Detached 2 men to 1st Feet Amb. in OVILLERS to supervise chlorination of water. Three + 4 men to an advanced post in AVELUY – each with an area beyond the R. ANCRE.	
"	22/8/16		" To OVILLERS re water & refuse.	
"	23/8/16		" To ALBERT re Bouzincourt water supply. To AVELUY & OVILLERS (Fritz's well).	
"	24/8/16		" To Crucifix corner & left sector trenches – fairly clean.	
"	25/8/16		" To AVELUY – To ALBERT to meet R.E. officer in charge water supply.	
"	26/8/16		" Visit of O.C. Lou Lee 25th Div relieving. To AMIENS – pay day at laundry. 144 Bde into line of route AUCHONVILLERS.	
"	27/8/16		" Preparing to move. Withdrawn men from AVELUY.	
"	28/8/16		" Withdrew water duty men from OVILLERS. MOVE to BUS area. To BUS & AUTHIE re baths.	
BUS	29/8/16		" To AUTHIE choosing site for bath for 143 Bde on R. AUTHIE.	
"	30/8/16		" Erecting bath at AUTHIE. Baths working at BUS.	

Bale Capt. R.A.M.C.

Army Form C.2118.

WAR DIARY
or
INTELLIGENCE SUMMARY
(Erase heading not required.)

Instructions regarding War Diaries and Intelligence Summaries are contained in F. S. Regs., Part II. and the Staff Manual respectively. Title Pages will be prepared in manuscript.

Place	Date	Hour	Summary of Events and Information	Remarks and references to Appendices
BUS	31/8/16		Routine. To BUS + AUTHIE.	

The Bn has been resting part of the month, when it was not difficult to make the sanitation satisfactory and to give the men baths & clean clothes, and moving and fighting for the remainder of the month.

In the area of the fighting sanitation was very difficult – but fortunately in and near the front line there was plenty of good water (in OVILLERS) and not very many house flies, though "blue bottles" were there in enormous numbers.

In the area of bivouacs and horse lines, flies were very prevalent owing to the large dumps of untreated horse manure.

The health of the troops has been fairly good except for many cases of P.U.O. and of diarrhoea – most of which however rapidly recovered.

Cases of infectious diseases reported — one case early of dysentery; Enteric Paratyphoid A and Cerebrospinal fever — two cases of scarlet fever. In no case has the source of infection been traced.

Lice are generally present but cases of extreme heavy infestation are not common. It is reported that when in captured dugouts, suffered severely from fleas but did not pick up many lice.

Capt RAMC T
Pole Capt RAMC T

2449 Wt. W14957/M90 750,000 1/16 J.B.C. & A. Forms/C.2118/12.

(Confidential)

War Diary
of
O.C. Sanitary Section - 48th (S.M.) Div
from
1st September 1916 to 30th September 1916.
(Volumn 18)

Vol 18

Sept 1916

COMMITTEE FOR THE
MEDICAL HISTORY OF THE WA[R]
Date 26 OCT 1915

Army Form C. 2118.

WAR DIARY
or
INTELLIGENCE SUMMARY
(Erase heading not required.)

Instructions regarding War Diaries and Intelligence Summaries are contained in F. S. Regs., Part II. and the Staff Manual respectively. Title Pages will be prepared in manuscript.

Place	Date	Hour	Summary of Events and Information	Remarks and references to Appendices
BUS	1/9/16		One Bde in trenches – two in Reserve. Section doing routine work. 8 men detailed with Bde H.Q. etc. O.C. to trenches opposite MAILLY – conditions good.	
"	2/9/16		Routine. To AMIENS – payday at Laundry DULEUX. Capt Bayley BUTLER RAMC arrives to take over Baths and Laundry.	
"	3/9/16		Routine. Divl H.Qrs move to BEAUVAL. To Laundry with AAQMG.	
"	4/9/16		" To SUCRERIE by COLINCAMPS to test water supply to trenches.	
"	5/9/16		" Fixed disinfector at Baths BUS to sterilize outer clothing whilst men bath and change underclothes.	
"	6/9/16		" To EOUIN, MARIEUX, VAUCHELLES	
"	7/9/16		"	
"	8/9/16		" To AUTHIE inspecting RE Billets. Meeting of Sanitary Officers at DDMS Office MARIEUX	
"	9/9/16		" To Laundry with Capt BUTLER 4/c.	
"	10/9/16		" Section moves to BEAUVAL, Brigades to BEAUVAL, GEZAINCOURT & ORVILLE areas.	
BEAUVAL	11/9/16		Routine. To BUS.	
"	12/9/16		" To GEZAINCOURT. One case Dysentery 241 Bde R.F.A.	
"	13/9/16		" To AMPLIER & ORVILLE. Training Salvage by men as sanitary orderlies – 2 for each M.G. Coy.	
"	14/9/16		" To GEZAINCOURT & AUTHVILLE re Relief to proposed laundry.	
"	15/9/16		" To AMPLIER & ORVILLE. Detached Cpl to assist Town Major	
"	16/9/16		" W.W. DATING to GEZAINCOURT, AMPLIER & ORVILLE. One case Dysentery 1/6 Bn R.W.R. Wale Capt RAMC o/c.	

2449 Wt. W14957/Mgo 750,000 1/16 J.B.C. & A. Forms/C.2118/12.

Army Form C. 2118.

WAR DIARY
or
INTELLIGENCE SUMMARY

(Erase heading not required.)

Instructions regarding War Diaries and Intelligence Summaries are contained in F.S. Regs., Part II and the Staff Manual respectively. Title Pages will be prepared in manuscript.

Place	Date	Hour	Summary of Events and Information	Remarks and references to Appendices
BEAUVAL	17/9/16		Routine. To BERNAVILLE preparatory to move.	
BERNAVILLE	18/9/16		Whole Div. (less Artillery still in action) moves to BERNAVILLE — 'A' area.	
"	19/9/16		Routine. One case Dysentery 1/8 Bn R. War. R.	
"	20/9/16		" Lecture to Officers + N.C.O.'s of all battalions begun with 1/5 + 1/6 Bn R. War R.	
"	21/9/16		" One case Typhoid 1/3 Sn Fd Amb. One Typhoid 241 B⁵ R.F.A. One Enteric Div Ammn Col.	
"			Lecture to 1/4 + 8 Bn R. War. R.	
"	22/9/16		" One case dysentery 1/4 Gloster	
"	23/9/16		" Lecture to 1/4 Bn Gloster	
"			To LE MEILLARD & OUTRE BOIS.	
"	24/9/16		" Lecture to 8th Bn Worcesters	
"	25/9/16		" To CANDAS & FIENVILLERS. Lecture to 1/4 Bn Ox⁰ & Bucks L.I.	
"	26/9/16		" Lecture to 1/6 Bn Glosters & 1/4 Bn R. Berks. One case Typhoid 1/6 Bn R. War Reg⁰.	
"	27/9/16		" Detached 2 men to Town Major CANDAS, FIENVILLERS. Lecture to 1/5 Gloster	
"			one case dysentery 6 Glosters, one case dysentery 240th B⁵ R.F.A.	
"	28/9/16		" Lecture to Bucks Bn. Oxf⁰ & B⁰ L.I. One case dysentery 1/4 Gloster.	
"	29/9/16		" Lecture to 1/4 Worcesters One dysentery 243 B⁵ R.F.A.	
"	30/9/16		" Move to HENU + area. Taking over from O.C. Sanitation 33rd Div'n.	
			To SOUASTRE re baths. 1 case ? Typhoid 1/4 Ox⁰ & Bucks L.I. 1 case ? Dysentery	
				240 th B⁵ R.F.A.

Dale Capt R.A.M.C.

WAR DIARY or INTELLIGENCE SUMMARY

Army Form C. 2118.

Place	Date	Hour	Summary of Events and Information	Remarks and references to Appendices
	September "16"		Except for the first 10 days of the month when the Div'n had one Bde in the line the Div'n has been resting and training and has moved three times. The artillery has been in action on the Somme and is rejoining at the end of the month. In the REAUVAL and the BERNAVILLE areas - when there were few or no really existing sanitary arrangements - field sanitation with straddle trench latrines has largely resorted to and was fairly well done.

The health of the troops has been fairly good with a continuance of the cases of P.U.O. mostly of short duration as noted last month and an increase of diarrhoea most of the cases of which yielded readily to treatment. 14 cases of the enteric group have been notified, eleven of these since 20th inst, viz 3 typhoid, 1 typhoid (enteric group), 9 dysentery. Of these 2 dysenteries from the 1/6 R War R, 9 9 from 240th Bde R.F.A. The remainder from separate units. No information has been received, (although asked for,) as to the type of dysentery.

Flies were very prevalent in the early part of the month.

There has been ample opportunity for bathing the men - hot showers baths having been available in 8 villages - several in each area - and there has been ample clothing from the laundry to change each man's underclothes at least twice. Lice are still prevalent but the degree of infestation is slight. | |

F. Dale, Capt R.A.M.C.
D.A.D.M.S.

140/1767

418th Divl Sanitary Section

Apl 1916

Oct 1916

COMMITTEE FOR THE
MEDICAL HISTORY OF THE WAR
Date -2 DEC. 1916

(Confidential)

Vol 19

War Diary
of
N. Sanitary Section 48th (S.M.) Div.
from
1st October 1916 to 31st October 1916

(Volume 19)

WAR DIARY
or
INTELLIGENCE SUMMARY
(Erase heading not required.)

Army Form C. 2118.

Place	Date	Hour	Summary of Events and Information	Remarks and references to Appendices
HENU	1/10/16		Section arrived in new area. Six N.C.O's were detached with R.E. H.Qrs. Routine O.C. to WARLINCOURT – Town major & batmen.	
"	2/10/16		Routine. Div. Artillery rejoin but from Somme. 1 N.C.O. detached to Town major WARLINCOURT.	
"	3/10/16		Capt. Butler Rtn'd Yc. Bath leaves handed over Baths & Laundry. With Major Wakelin S/ARMS. Sanitation Thro' Army to ST. AMAND & SOUASTRE.	
"	4/10/16		To Souastre, Bouileux, Amiens. 2 N.C.O's detached to Town Major FONQUEVILLERS, one N.C.O. to Town Major ST. AMAND, one to SOUASTRE.	
"	5/10/16		To BAYENCOURT, ST AMAND & SOUASTRE. One N.C.O. to Town Major MONDICOURT.	
"	6/10/16		To HEBUTERNE with rations.	
"	7/10/16		To AMIENS – Pay day at Civil Laundry.	
"	8/10/16		To SOUASTRE re dysentery cases notified in V/4 Worcesters.	
"	9/10/16		To ST AMAND, SOUASTRE and LA HAIE.	
"	10/10/16		To LA HAIE and SOUASTRE. Set up disinfecting apparatus at SOUASTRE Baths capable of 600 blankets per day.	
"	11/10/16		To FONQUEVILLERS, SOUASTRE & ST AMAND.	
"	12/10/16		SOUASTRE, ST AMAND & WARLINCOURT.	
"	13/10/16		To SOUASTRE re case Shiga dysentery in 5th Bn Lincs. To ST AMAND. Visit of new M.O. 320th Bde R.F.A.	
"	14/10/16		To AMIENS – Pay day at Civ. Laundry. N.C.O. return from MONDICOURT on relief by another B.W.	
"	15/10/16		To SOUASTRE. One N.C.O to Town Major HUMBERCOURT.	

F. Dale Capt. R.A.M.C.
O/C.

Army Form C. 2118.

WAR DIARY
or
INTELLIGENCE SUMMARY
(Erase heading not required.)

Instructions regarding War Diaries and Intelligence Summaries are contained in F. S. Regs., Part II. and the Staff Manual respectively. Title Pages will be prepared in manuscript.

Place	Date	Hour	Summary of Events and Information	Remarks and references to Appendices
HENU	16/10/16		Routine. To AMIENS - Laundry	
"	17/10/16		" To SOUASTRE, ST AMAND and HUMBERCOURT.	
"	18/10/16		" To PAS. - RSMs Corps. Visit of C. Laurie, PM. RSW	
"	19/10/16		" 3 N.C.O. detached to Town Major SAILLY, BAYENCOURT, & HEBUTERNE to relieve N.C.O's of Same Rgt RSW	
"	20/10/16		" Visit of O.C. Sam section 49th DW to relieve us	
"	21/10/16		" Move to DOULLENS. All men attached to Town Majors relieved by 189th DW except those at WARLINCOURT & HUMBERCOURT.	
DOULLENS	22/10/16		"	
"	23/10/16		" Move to BAISIEUX - III Corps N.C.O. withdrawn from WARLINCOURT & HUMBERCOURT.	
BAISIEUX	24/10/16		Routine. Taking over from Le Wilson RAMC. charge of "A" Sanitary Area III Corps - the villages MIRVAUX, BEAUCOURT, BAYELINCOURT, BAISIEUX, HENENCOURT, MILLENCOURT and interviewing counsels	
"	25/10/16		" To HENENCOURT - III Corps Camp Commandant & MILLENCOURT - Town Major.	MILLENCOURT
"	26/10/16		" one staff sgt & 3 N.C.O. detached to Camp Commandant III Corps. Three N.C.O. to Town Major.	
"	27/10/16		" To BEAUCOURT & BAYELINCOURT, To HENENCOURT.	
"	28/10/16		" To AMIENS - Payday & Laundry.	
"	29/10/16		" To MIRVAUX. - detached one N.C.O. and working party of 3 men to Town Major.	
"	30/10/16		" To HENENCOURT - RSMs.	
"	31/10/16		" To ALBERT with TAA & Q.M.S. re clothing store & traits. To camp of RW. H.Q. Quarters MILLENCOURT.	MILLENCOURT

V. Sale Capt. RAMC CF

WAR DIARY or INTELLIGENCE SUMMARY

Army Form C. 2118.

Place	Date	Hour	Summary of Events and Information	Remarks and references to Appendices
	October 1916		The Div's was holding the line with one Bt'n in trenches and two in reserve in VII Corps area until the 21st of the month, when it moved to DOULLENS area for two days and then to III Corps reserve area. The willow remained in the line under VII Corps.	
			Sanitation in VII Corps area was very difficult owing to the congestion of the area. It was very wet weather and the frequent moves of units. The latrine system there was that of ground latrines and incinerator pits – and under the care of the Town Major. The incinerators were very difficult owing to the wet wood. It was fairly well carried out. The units in entrenched camps and bivouacs outside the villages had to resort to straddle trenches – but these were spoiled by disuse as fast as solitary users could be constructed. Biscuit tins were used in the trenches. In the III Corps area the system is that of deep pits with fly proof seats.	
			The health of the troops has been better this last month. The diarrhoea having greatly diminished. There have been known as large a number of cases of Pyrexia U.O. months unknown. Notifications of infectious disease have been higher than ever before. 25 enteric group were notified including 5 cases of typhoid, 5 cases Para A, 4 Cases Para B, one dip'th'a dysentery, 3 Febrile dysentery and Dysentery of unknown origin. Almost all of these were had pre sick in late August or early Sept and who pretty infected when Div was in the Somme battle area. All Enteric were very severe cases of diarrhoea with blood, of which many had a number, in stept - 1 case stayed ill on 1/9/16 when no dysentery was diagnosed - although urgent to. There were also notified 3 cases of diphtheria, 1 scarlet fever, 1 measles, 3 german measles and 3 of mumps. there was civilian mumps in the village of WARLINCOURT. The sanitary fatigues are always plenty of clean clothes. The privative out means or powders available	

Dale Cpt. RAMC

140/1846

(Confidential)

War Diary

of Sanitary Section 48th (S.M.) Div=

from

1st November 1916 to 30th November 1916

(Volume 20)

Vol 20

COMMITTEE FOR THE
MEDICAL HISTORY OF THE WAR
Date −3 JAN. 1917

WAR DIARY
or
INTELLIGENCE SUMMARY

Army Form C. 2118.

Place	Date	Hour	Summary of Events and Information	Remarks and references to Appendices
BAIZIEUX	1/4/16		Section working in "A" Area III Corps as already described. 10 men detached with Town Major, one with DWE HQrs, one with III Corps HQrs and one at DWE Laundry. Routine work. O.C. to camps between MILLENCOURT and ALBERT.	
"	2/4/16		To HENENCOURT, MILLENCOURT and camps beyond. 4 men detached to supervise camps end of MILLENCOURT and to billet there. 2 P.B men sent from BAIZIEUX to Town Major MIRVAUX and two to Town Major BAYEL + BEAUCOURT.	
"	3/4/16		To ALBERT (clothing store & disinfecting station) + DWE Hd Qrs at FRICOURT.	
"	4/4/16		To DWE Laundry at SALEUX.	
"	5/4/16			
"	6/4/16		To DMS IV Army. To DDMS III Corps Office - conference of dun. Offrs with San Off IV Army.	
"	7/4/16		To DWE Hd Qrs - for indent for wood shovels.	
"	8/4/16		To ALBERT - clothing store.	
"	9/4/16		To TSEAUCOURT + MIRVAUX.	
"	10/4/16		To HENENCOURT + HENENCOURT WOOD CAMP.	
"	11/4/16		To DWE Laundry SALEUX.	
"	12/4/16		Gave N.C.O. Esq 44th Inf. Bde.	
"	13/4/16		To HENENCOURT, MILLENCOURT + ALBERT.	
"	14/4/16			

Dale Capt RAMC

Army Form C. 2118.

WAR DIARY
or
INTELLIGENCE SUMMARY
(Erase heading not required.)

Instructions regarding War Diaries and Intelligence Summaries are contained in F. S. Regs., Part II. and the Staff Manual respectively. Title Pages will be prepared in manuscript.

Place	Date	Hour	Summary of Events and Information	Remarks and references to Appendices
BAIZIEUX	15th		Routine. O.C. goes on leave U.K. — O.C. 2nd S.M. Fd Amb. takes charge of section	
"	16th		"	
"	17th		"	
"	18th		"	
"	19th		" — strict of strength	
"	20th		" Three men detached from section to go to form new sanitary section for ALBERT — under orders D.D.M.S. III Corps.	
"	21st		"	
"	22nd		"	
"	23rd		"	
"	24th		"	
"	25th		"	
"	26th		"	
"	27th		" OC returned from leave.	
"	28th		" To HENENCOURT — D.D.M.S. Office. Area rearranged so that WARLOY, HADENCOURT, CONTAY, PIERREGOT, MOLLIENS are added to A area which no longer includes BAIZIEUX, BEAUCOURT and RAVELINCOURT.	
"	29th		" To WARLOY.	
"	30th		" To ALBERT — clothing stores disinfector. To WARLOY.	

Wade Capt R.A.M.C.
O/c

Army Form C. 2118.

WAR DIARY
or
INTELLIGENCE SUMMARY
(Erase heading not required.)

Instructions regarding War Diaries and Intelligence Summaries are contained in F. S. Regs., Part II. and the Staff Manual respectively. Title Pages will be prepared in manuscript.

Place	Date	Hour	Summary of Events and Information	Remarks and references to Appendices
	November 1916		During the month the Divs has been holding the line by LE SARS & EAUCOURT L'ABBAYE and the sanitary section which became Corps Troops at the end of Oct. has been separated from the Divs. Consequently it is not possible to comment on the sanitation, the health business etc of the Divs as before. The section has continued in charge of the disinfection of clothing and the laundry as before and this has been working satisfactorily. To judge from the state of the clothing lice continue to be prevalent. Notification of infectious diseases have been received which show that 26 cases of the following group have been notified including 5 cases of typhoid, 7 of Paratyphoid A, 4 of Paratyphoid B, 8 of Flexner Dysentery and 2 of Dysentery S.H.O. There have also been notified one case of Cerebro spinal meningitis, two cases of Diphtheria, and one case of Mumps.

The system of putting sanitary sections in charge of areas irrespective of what troops occupy them seems to work well in so far as – since forming in centres in the various villages and a central workshop in the area can make sanitary fittings, equipment unhindered by moves.

The state of the villages and camps in the area is satisfactory on the whole except in the villages recently taken over.

Dale Lt Col RAMC
i/c San Sec 48 Div | |

Vol 21

149/900

Confidential

War Diary
of
O i/c Sanitary Section 48th S. M. Div.

from
1st Dec. 1916 to 31st Dec 1916

(Volume 21)

COMMITTEE FOR THE
MEDICAL HISTORY OF THE WAR
Date 31 JAN.1917

Army Form C. 2118.

WAR DIARY
or
INTELLIGENCE SUMMARY
(Erase heading not required.)

Instructions regarding War Diaries and Intelligence Summaries are contained in F. S. Regs., Part II. and the Staff Manual respectively. Title Pages will be prepared in manuscript.

Place	Date	Hour	Summary of Events and Information	Remarks and references to Appendices
WARLOY	1 12/16		Section in charge of Area III Corps – with HQrs & workshops in WARLOY and 14 men detached with Town Major of the other village in the Warloy Routine work. Section also in charge of laundry & disinfection of clothing of 48th Div.	
"	2 12/16		O.e. To laundry at SALEUX	
"	3 12/16		" To MILLENCOURT & HENENCOURT	
"	4 12/16		" To CONTAY – to S.W. clothing store ALBERT – SG Dump	
"	5 12/16		" To MOLLIENS au BOIS – To HENENCOURT – to S.W. school ST GRATIEN	
"	6 12/16		Inspection of WARLOY with Town Major	
"	7 12/16		Testing water supplies at WARLOY. Conference with M.O. & of Field Amb. WARLOY	
"	8 12/16		To CONTAY – To HENENCOURT	
"	9 12/16		To S.W. Laundry	
"	10 12/16		To Corps HQrs	
"	11 12/16		To ALBERT – clothing store & disinfector – & HENENCOURT – Fitting disinfector for 150 blankets per day at Fd Amb. WARLOY	
"	12 12/16		To MOLLIENS, PIERREGOT & CONTAY	
"	13 12/16		To CONTAY to make report on case of rabies there	
"	14 12/16		[signature] Lt Col RAMC

2449 Wt. W14957/M90 750,000 1/16 J.B.C. & A. Forms/C.2118/12.

WAR DIARY
or
INTELLIGENCE SUMMARY

(Erase heading not required.)

Army Form C. 2118.

Place	Date	Hour	Summary of Events and Information	Remarks and references to Appendices
WARLOY	15/12/16		Routine Work. — To VADENCOURT lecture & inspecting water supplies. To HENENCOURT.	
"	16/12/16	"	To Divl Laundry.	
"	17/12/16	"	To HENENCOURT — MILLENCOURT — To ALBERT — clothing store, for AD Q2A.	
"	18/12/16	"	Inspection with DDMS in WARLOY & VADENCOURT. To HENENCOURT.	
"	19/12/16	"	Report to DDMS, on lack of disinfecting arrangements — suggesting the setting up of disinfecting stations in suitable centres.	
"	20/12/16	"	To HENENCOURT, MILLENCOURT corps Rec'd W/s — ALBERT, arrival of 3 reinforcements from 1st Lon. Terr. Coy.	
"	21/12/16	"	O.C. Influenza.	
"	22/12/16	"	"	
"	23/12/16	"	To HENENCOURT.	
"	24/12/16	"	To Divl Laundry.	
"	25/12/16	"	Christmas Day. To ALBERT.	
"	26/12/16	"	To Divl Laundry.	
"	27/12/16	"	To ALBERT — Clothing store & Disinfector. To MILLENCOURT & HENENCOURT	
"	28/12/16	"	To MOLLIENS-AU-BOIS and Divl Laundry. + HENENCOURT WOOD CAMP.	
"	29/12/16	"	To Army Hd Qrs re lectures Army School of Sanitation at ALBERT to Corps HQ Qu-Bois-re,	
"	30/12/16	"	Preparing for School of Instruction.	
"	31/12/16	"		

Dale Capt RAMC
4C

WAR DIARY or INTELLIGENCE SUMMARY

Army Form C. 2118.

Place	Date	Hour	Summary of Events and Information	Remarks and references to Appendices

During the month the Sanitary Section i/c A. area III Corps has again been separated from the Div: except that 1 man has been att'd to Div: H.Q. and 1 to 144 Fd H.Q. and that the section has supervised disinfection of clothes and the Laundry. The disinfection and laundry have both been working satisfactorily except for some delay owing to mechanical breakdown at the laundry.

The sanitation of A. area has been satisfactory on the whole and a large number (40) latrines mostly of trench and fabrication trenches (?) have been made and erected in the various villages of the area. The billets in the village are in a pretty good state though material is very difficult to obtain and many small repairs to roofs and walls still require to be done. The chief hindrance to making the men reasonably comfortable in the canvas camps and the camps in the open is the appallingly muddy state of the ground.

Cases of infections disease notified in the Div. during the month shows a further increase on previous month viz 34 cases of Enteric group against 26 in November and 25 in October. These 34 cases include 32 cases of Dysentery (24 Flexner, 4 Shiga, 1 unusual & 3 of unknown origin) 3 Enteric group, one Para A and 1 Para B. If dysentery cases occurred in one Battalion, 8 in another, 4 in each of two other battalions — in other words 21 of 32 cases occurred in 4 battalions and 4 battalions were without any cases. There were also notified 5 cases of diphtheria all in different platoons of the same Battalion and the 1 case of Mumps.

Dale Capt R.A.M.C. San Off.
48 Div.

140/1947

48th Divl. Sanitary Section.

COMMITTEE FOR THE
MEDICAL HISTORY OF THE WAR
Date 13 MAR. 1917

Army Form C. 2118.

WAR DIARY
or
INTELLIGENCE SUMMARY.
(Erase heading not required.)

Vol 22

CONFIDENTIAL

War Diary
of
Sanitary Section
48th Division

from 1-1-17 to 31-1-17.

Army Form C. 2118.

WAR DIARY
or
INTELLIGENCE SUMMARY.
(Erase heading not required.)

Instructions regarding War Diaries and Intelligence Summaries are contained in F. S. Regs., Part II. and the Staff Manual respectively. Title pages will be prepared in manuscript.

Place	Date	Hour	Summary of Events and Information	Remarks and references to Appendices
MORLAY	1/4/17		Sanitary Section in charge of "A" Coln III Corps overlooking of villages of MOLLIENS-AU-BOIS, CONTAY, VADENCOURT, WARLOY, HENENCOURT, BAIZEUX & the adjoining neighbourhood. Headquarters of Section & workshop at WARLOY.	
			Fourteen O.R. Detached for Sanitary Duties with the 7 am Brigade the same village as this one.	
			O.C. proceeded from the Staff H.Q. & Army behind 1/3 mountain rest.	
WARLOY	2/4/17		Water Laid in the village & water bottles filled by R.E. of a pumping Engine.	
"	3/4/17		1 A.C.O. attached from Regt MOLLIENS returned sent to village.	
"	4/4/17		Gave extra Latrines fixed in the village.	
"	5/4/17		6/4/15 in WARLOY inspected. Found in good sanitary condition.	
"	6/4/17		All attached men called upon here of quarters in response of new orders.	
"			Visited Divisional Sanitary Officer BAIZEUX.	
"	7/4/17		Local women to work in this village approving his appointed.	
"	8/4/17		Staff Sgt Barren attached Annual with III Corps Headquarters.	
			Billets of the Section handed over to Sanitary Section of 2nd Div on m 8 Sunday.	
			Officer & finish h. taking on control of the area.	

Army Form C. 2118.

WAR DIARY
or
INTELLIGENCE SUMMARY.
(Erase heading not required.)

Instructions regarding War Diaries and Intelligence Summaries are contained in F.S. Regs., Part II. and the Staff Manual respectively. Title pages will be prepared in manuscript.

Place	Date	Hour	Summary of Events and Information	Remarks and references to Appendices
WARLOY	9.1.17	10 am	Entrained Section for HALLENCOURT.	
		3 pm	Section arrived at HALLENCOURT.	
HALLENCOURT	10.1.17		3 ORs attached to each Bye HQrs for carrying duties supervising the sanitation of battalions	
	11.1.17 – 12.1.17		Routine work, & visiting various villages	
	13.1.17		Visited HIERCOURT, inspecting & visiting various cafés. There is a great lack of incinerators & latrines in this area. OUDENENT, AIRAINES & HUPPY which are claiming attention	
	14.1.17		MERELESSART visited & sanitary arrangements inspected inst. 1/19 R.W.F. & 9	
	15.1.17		Visited NEUVILLE & 145 B.F. HQrs questions	
	16.1.17		Visited CERISY-BULEUX. Inspected 49 billets at AIRAINES - sanitary arrangements	
	17.1.17		Routine work	
	18.1.17		Visited & made attempts to find PONT-REMY - found satisfactory	
	19.1.17		Routine work	
	20.1.17		Routine work	
	21.1.17		Work at AIRAINES visited - found satisfactory	

Army Form C. 2118.

WAR DIARY
or
INTELLIGENCE SUMMARY.
(Erase heading not required.)

Instructions regarding War Diaries and Intelligence Summaries are contained in F.S. Regs., Part II. and the Staff Manual respectively. Title pages will be prepared in manuscript.

Place	Date	Hour	Summary of Events and Information	Remarks and references to Appendices
HALLENCOURT	22/1/17		Visited FRUCOURT with reference to location of urinals & latrines. Reconnoitred	
"	23/1/17 & 24/1/17		billets of 144th Inf. and sighted Battery at FRUCOURT	
			Routine work.	
"	25/1/17		Inspected billets at BOREL & tested water supply.	
"	26/1/17		Routine work.	
"	27/1/17		Men from 143 Bde. employed in preparation for moving into a new area forward	
"	28/1/17	10 a.m.	Section entrained for MERICOURT-SUR-SOMME, where division is taking over from the French.	
		2 p.m.	Section arrived at MERICOURT.	
"	29/1/17		3 OR attached to 143 Infy. Brigade - 144th Infy. Bde. at CERISY-GAILLY and 145th Infantry Brigade at HAMEL. The Sanitary condition of these villages & camps in neighbourhood is bad - being a great lack of incinerators & Inspection Latrines. Instructions issued to Battalion Medical Officers regarding the	
"	30/1/17 - 31/1/17		Routine work & instructions issued to Battalion Medical Officers regarding the construction of latrines & testing water supplies.	

J.J.K. Beckh
Capt. R.A.M.C.
For O.C. 48th Sanitary Section

140/99 4

Vol 76
#5

Confidential.

War Diary
of
O/c Sanitary Section 48th/SM/DIV=
from 1st Feb to 28th Feb. 1917
(Volume 23)

Feb. 1917

COMMITTEE FOR THE
...CAL HISTORY OF THE WAR
Date 4.— APR. 1917

Army Form C. 2118.

WAR DIARY
or
INTELLIGENCE SUMMARY.
(Erase heading not required.)

Instructions regarding War Diaries and Intelligence Summaries are contained in F. S. Regs., Part II. and the Staff Manual respectively. Title pages will be prepared in manuscript.

Place	Date	Hour	Summary of Events and Information	Remarks and references to Appendices
MERICOURT	1-2-17		Divl HQ moving - Division taking over line from French.	
"	2.2.17		Scarletta in chateau being improved. Generally the sanitation fall camps unsatisfactory	
"	3.2.17		Sanitary Section moved to Cappy	
CAPPY	4.2.17.		Inspected sanitation of CAPPY which is bad. Workshops are mapped out.	
"	5.2.17		Sites for latrines in the village chosen. System for collection & the burning of contents instituted	
"	6.2.17		Visited the area generally of the Division. The sanitation is very poor & needs a great deal of attention. Town Majors interviewed.	
CAPPY	6/2/17		Baths arrived at CAPPY and ECLUSIER	
"	7/2/17		Visit to HERBECOURT. Water at CAPPY it too and found to be if good/any	
"	8/2/17		Visit to FLAUCOURT. Water at 144" Inf Bde. & 2nd " Bde. RFA.	
"	9/2/17		Visit to ECLUSIER and FRISE.	
"	10/2/17		Visit to 145th Inf Bde in trenches. Consolidation areas by the French very bad.	
"	11/2/17		Visit to FROISSY and Camp OLYMPE	
"	12/2/17		Visit to MARLY Camp and report thereon	
"	13/2/17		Visit to Northern battery positions. Suggestions as to water supply thereof	
"	14/2/17		Visit to CAPPY and Artillery wagon lines	

J Davidson
Capt R.A.M.C.

Army Form C. 2118.

WAR DIARY
or
INTELLIGENCE SUMMARY.
(Erase heading not required.)

Instructions regarding War Diaries and Intelligence Summaries are contained in F. S. Regs., Part II. and the Staff Manual respectively. Title pages will be prepared in manuscript.

Place	Date	Hour	Summary of Events and Information	Remarks and references to Appendices
CAPPY	15/9/17		Visit to Camp 56 & Fouruche, to be greatly improved	
	16/9/17		Visit to 143rd Inf. Bde. Very little improvements have been carried out. Recommendations made as to action. Water point in front of FLAUCOURT useless, and one of artillery advanced fitting point condemned. Recommendations to Town Major ECLUSIER.	
	17/9/17		Visit to January. 1 man detached from CAPPY to Town Major ECLUSIER.	
	18/9/17		Investigation of a case of Measles at FROISSY. Visit to MARLY Camp — 2 men attached to Town Major FLAUCOURT	
	19/9/17		Visit to Camp Commandant MARLY. Inspection of CAPPY.	
	20/9/17		Visit to O.Y.B. Bltn. re cases of Measles. 1 man attached to T.M. Camp 56	
	21/9/17		Visit to Southern gun position, Sophie Trenet, and P.C. Tourbon.	
	22/9/17		Visit to ECLUSIER and round CAPPY.	
	23/9/17		Visit to FROISSY and CAPPY.	
	24/9/17		Routine — Visit with Capt Davidson Rame to Herbecourt, Flaucourt, & 240 B.&.R.F.A. — also Cappy	A) Davidson Capt. R.H.M.T.
	25/9/17		" to BRAY — with A.D.M.S. & A.A.& Q.M.G. to MARLY CAMP & FROISSY	
	26/9/17		" with D.A.& Q.M.G. to O.B. Railhead, FROISSY, CAPPY, ECLUSIER, FRISE & Camps.	
	27/9/17		" to HERBECOURT & FLAUCOURT — Town Major. With Capt. T. McMahon Hygiene Lab. to Whitbread 2 men attached to T.M. ECLUSIER	
	28/9/17		" To Camp 56 & ECLUSIER 1 day 9 men attached to T.M. ECLUSIER in Village & Camps.	Dale Capt. R.A.M.C. O.Y.C.

T.1134. Wt. W708—776. 500000. 4/15. Sir J. C. & S.

Confidential

War Diary.
of
O.C. Sanitary Section - 48th (Sm.) Division.
from March 1/1917 to March 31/17.
(Volume 34)

140/2043.

Vol 34

Nov 1917

COMMITTEE FOR THE
MEDICAL HISTORY OF THE WAR
Date 11 MAY 1917

Army Form C. 2118.

WAR DIARY
or
INTELLIGENCE SUMMARY.
(Erase heading not required.)

Place	Date	Hour	Summary of Events and Information	Remarks and references to Appendices
CAPPY	1/3/17		Division holding front opposite PERONNE and occupying area along southside of Somme Canal as far west as FROISSY. Headquarters and workshop of section. 1 - CAPPY: M.1. NCO & 3 men, attached Town Major HERBECOURT-FLAVICOURT. One Sgt. and 4 a/cpls. attached Town Major ECLUSIER for village and neighbouring camps. One a/cpl & 1 man attached Town-Major MARLY-FROISSY. One Staff Sgt. attached VII Corps HQrs, 1 a/staff sgt. attached VII Corps HQrs. One man at DWE Laundry. 1 man (an Indian) engaged on exam. of water carts & water points.	
	2/3/17		Routine work. Visit to Camp 52 and water points there and at point G.15.c.32. G.R.1a central, G.21d central, G.25a83 Map 62d.	
	3/3/17		Routine. Installation of Naval Chlorination apparatus at water point Flaucle L'Eglise CAPPY.	
	4/3/17	"	Visit to Hygiene Lab. taking water samples from FLAVICOURT & HERBECOURT. Visit to Fourth Army medical soc. paper on Dysentery.	
	5/3/17	"	Camps 56, 50 bis, 60 & ECLUSIER - recommendation. Post-mortem on indian death in 1/6 R Warr R at Maurepas Ravine.	
	6/3/17	"	Visit of O.C. Sam. Sec, 61st Div, W.I.T.D.Q & R.Q.M.G. 5th Divn. - FROISSY, ECLUSIER, Camp 62, & CAPPY. Take Capt TRANCH O/c.	

WAR DIARY or INTELLIGENCE SUMMARY.

Army Form C. 2118.

Place	Date	Hour	Summary of Events and Information	Remarks and references to Appendices
CAPPY	7/3/17		Routine. Visit to HERBECOURT, Water Supply C.35.d.53, 4th Gordons 8th Worcs & A.T.S. in trenches.	
CAPPY	8/3/17		" Visit to HERBECOURT, Vaux. To Div Laundry.	
"	9/3/17		" " To Div Train.	
"	10/3/17		" C.R.E. Camp 51. Camp 50 bis to ECLUSIER.	
"	11/3/17		" " At ECLUSIER & Camp 56.	
"	12/3/17		" Lectures to N.C.Os & men of Sanitary sqds of each of units – all of whom are to be sent to Van Lee for 2 days. Visit to Canal Bank A Camp Lecture as above. Handing over section to Capt Buchanan R.A.M.C. now appointed to Command.	
"	13/3/17		"	
"	14/3/17.		" Assumed Command of Unit. Lecture to NCOs and men of Sanitary Squads of Units. Visited area occupied by "B" Battery 242 Bde R.F.A. occupied by Units of 145 Inf Bde bat CAPPY. Artillery improvement made by Mr Bde R.F.A. Recommendations forwarded re Prevalence of Scabies.	Saw Capt Russell (aff= R.A.M.S. team Fourth Army) inspected trestles
	15/3/17.			

T.J.134. Wt. W708—776. 500000. 4/15. Sir J. C. & S.

WAR DIARY
or
INTELLIGENCE SUMMARY.
(Erase heading not required.)

Army Form C. 2118.

Place	Date	Hour	Summary of Events and Information	Remarks and references to Appendices
CAPPY	16/3/17		Talking to NCOs and men of Sanitary Squads, Latrines and incinerators at CAPPY. T.M. CAPPY refused to provide fatigue for removal of latrines. Further lecture to NCOs. Then	
	17/3/17		Sanitary Squads in afternoon. Lectures to NCOs and men of Sanitary Squads of Units. Shoes taken over, village and camp for frequent inspection. Camp 56 visited. Various defects noted and recommendations made.	
	18/3/17		Visited Biaches, La Maisonette and outskirts of La Chapelette to investigate state of battlefield lie in area evacuated by Germans. Report of investigation reported to A.D.M.S.	
	19/3/17		Further investigation of battlefield in area evacuated by enemy at O.8.d.37, O.9.c.7, 69.a.33. La Chapelette I.33.d.52 and HALLE. Result of investigation reports to A.D.M.S.	
	20/3/17		Investigation of water supplies PERONNE. Samples collected in previous day examined. Report forwarded to A.D.M.S.	

WAR DIARY
or
INTELLIGENCE SUMMARY

Army Form C. 2118.

Place	Date	Hour	Summary of Events and Information	Remarks and references to Appendices
CAPPY	21/3/17		Routine. Visited O.8.d.3.7. O.9.c.27. O.9.a.33. La Chapellette also I.33.d.20 & PERONNE & HALLE. All wells in these areas were appropriately labelled. Also visited ST RADEGENDE where No. 1 well was found and with [further?] trouble others intact. Above samples examined — waited for Visited CAPPY village and Camp. Be visited to NCOs & men of Sanitary Squads.	
	22/3/17		Routine lectures to NCOs and men of Sanitary Squads. Visited Cerisy and Rifle. Hammond discussed of Sanitary Wagon from Velletot. Proceeded with to BARLEUX. in Laboratory. Large interrogation to RE inclines was transport. No trials. A Maylords & Expenses present.	
	23/3/17		Routine lectures to NCOs & men of Sanitary Squads. Stores carried ready to by lorries on to [area?] to be provided by HWT. These lorries did not report — Stores and Equipment carried back to workshop again. Inspection of CAPPY and ascertained that it will	

WAR DIARY or INTELLIGENCE SUMMARY

Army Form C. 2118.

Place	Date	Hour	Summary of Events and Information	Remarks and references to Appendices
CAPPY	25/2/17 (contd)		W.O. left unsanitary condition of Boulogne troops. Moved to PERONNE. Examined specimens of water with them on call.	
PERONNE	26/3/17		Routine. Examined specimens of water at 1/1 Sm Fd Ambc. Sanitary work in PERONNE. Permit form III Corps for lorry to proceed CAPPY to PERONNE. Visited CAPPY. Forwarded Sulphuret to Major of staff by Lieut G. PERONNE. Examined Specimen of water from Pump at Rue de Paris bought it well in Rue de la Republique PERONNE. Both gave the reactions of Mayrio Control Experiments with the reagents alone gave similar reactions even more pro- nounced. Samples forwarded to ADMS to be sent to WO. Obviously incipients of nitric acid in Mayrio reagents. Cold bore at I. 28 a 52. Public latrine built I 27.6.34. Public latrine built I 27.6.24. Sample of water from well near church. Examined — was good	
Bentins	24/3/17			

WAR DIARY
or
INTELLIGENCE SUMMARY.
(Erase heading not required.)

Army Form C. 2118.

Place	Date	Hour	Summary of Events and Information	Remarks and references to Appendices
PERONNE	13/3/17		Routine. Lecture to NCO & men of Sanitary Squads. Visited the following area and collected wells details for Burke following points: DOINGT - Rush at I.35.b.88. Wells at I.36.a.41, I.36.a.64, I.36.a.74, I.29.d.38, I.36.a.central I.36.a.5c. COURCELLES. Well at I.30.c.66. Other wells broken. BUIRE. Stream J.27.d.88 - wells intact. TINCOURT. Wells at J.23.6.34, J.22.b.44, J.23.b.37, J.4.b.99. Probably many other wells in the village's be investigated later. Provisional report ADMS	
"	14/3/17		Routine. Lecture to NCO & Men of Sanitary Squads. Full report of above work supplied to ADMS. The construction of 4 furnaces & 2 ashes & 3 large incinerators to be complete. Improved incinerators built in open spaces of hilly shorty. Enormous accumulations of refuse in town. Visited RE	

WAR DIARY or INTELLIGENCE SUMMARY

Army Form C. 2118.

Place	Date	Hour	Summary of Events and Information	Remarks and references to Appendices
PERONNE	29/1/m/16	R.E.	Rough in PERONNE Latrine very unsatisfactory. Reported to ADMS. Refuse manure allowed to accumulate in town. Represented to ADMS. Town trapped.	
"	30/3		Venture visited RE Park with ADMS. Latrine condemned. New site recommended for both latrines & supplies to Sanitation. Useful following orders to work supplies — Bussu Well at I.18.b.71 (two wells one pump) T.13.a.11. I.18.670 T.13.651, I.18.652 DRIENCOURT Well at T.3.d.30 TEMPLEUX-la-FOSSE Wells at D.28.a.72, D.28.d.82, D.29.c.75. 1st well 152	
"	31/3	M.D.	LONG AVESNES — two wells found. Promised Captain to ADMO. Rubbish Latrines to ACD they Sanitary Squad. Further investigation of above well supplies. Report to ADMS. Visited Grenadguards in Section Nurnoras TINCOURT (I.24.a.6.4)or N BUCHAVESNES CUFFY ALLAIR De 18th Div. Sal Section	

www.ingramcontent.com/pod-product-compliance
Lightning Source LLC
Chambersburg PA
CBHW081552160426
43191CB00011B/1906